Welfare Mothers Speak Out

We Ain't Gonna Shuffle Anymore

Welfare Mothers Speak Out

We Ain't Gonna Shuffle Anymore

By the Milwaukee County Welfare Rights Organization

Mrs. Cassie B. Downer, Chairman
For the National Welfare Rights Organization

Thomas Howard Tarantino and Reverend Dismas Becker, Editors

Introduction by Dr. George A. Wiley, Executive Director,
National Welfare Rights Organization

W · W · NORTON & COMPANY · INC · NEW YORK

EC '73 0 0 8 2 0   /25
                     0945

Copyright © 1972 by W. W. Norton & Company, Inc.

FIRST EDITION
ALL RIGHTS RESERVED
Published simultaneously in Canada
by George J. McLeod Limited, Toronto

Library of Congress Cataloging in Publication Data

Milwaukee County Welfare Rights Organization.
Welfare mothers speak out.

Includes bibliographical references.
1. Public welfare—United States. 2. Economic
assistance, Domestic—United States. 3. Poor—United
States. I. Tarantino, Thomas Howard, ed. II. Becker,
Dismas, ed. III. Title.
HV95.M54   362.5'0973   72-3963
ISBN 0-393-01042-2
ISBN 0-393-01073-2 (pbk.)

Acknowledgment is gratefully extended to the following
for permission to reprint from their works: *Mad* Magazine,
© 1971, E. C. Publications, Inc.; Brumsic Brandon, Jr., for
"Luther"; and Lorenz, © 1971, The New Yorker Magazine
Inc.

PRINTED IN THE UNITED STATES OF AMERICA

1 2 3 4 5 6 7 8 9 0

Dedicated to
the majority of the American people

Contents

Contents

Foreword

Welfare mothers know what is going on in the world. They see all the lies and suffer all the abuses. It is time they were heard.

This book combines research conducted by the editors with the words—the knowledge—of the welfare mothers themselves. The research is of secondary importance, but it underlines what the mothers have to say; and what the mothers have to say is that you can't fool the people on the bottom.

—The Editors

Introduction

Everyone has the right to live. Yet, at this moment, 25.5 million Americans are living in the depths of poverty in the richest nation in the history of the world.

The United States spends over five times as much of the taxpayers' money for military costs as it does for the welfare of its people. As a per cent of national income, it spends less on welfare than any of sixteen European countries, and less than Canada, Israel, Australia, or New Zealand.

Politicians and newspapers publicize high welfare costs, but they ignore the fact that it costs ten times more to care for the physically stunted and mentally damaged victims of malnutrition than it would have cost to feed them as babies. And, even though the terms "hunger in America" and "welfare reform" are inseparable, when we hear those words we somehow form different impressions.

The fight for an adequate income for all Americans has been a long one, and it is far from over. The small victories that began with the march on Washington in 1963, continued through the civil rights movement, touched a nation's conscience with CBS's "Hunger in America," and flourished through the dedicated efforts of concerned citizens on all levels in all parts of the country are in constant danger of being wiped out by those who insist on putting money before people, by those who are determined to maintain the poor as a source of cheap labor.

Every American family of four should be guaranteed an adequate income of $6,500 a year. This is the government's own estimate of what is needed to provide a family with the bare essentials of life: food, clothing, shelter, health care, and transportation. Many people feel it is too high. Yet it is not extravagant. It is simply adequate.

In this book, the welfare mothers of America tell what poverty is really like . . . how it feels to be subjected to the indignities and dehumanization of the welfare system . . . how billions of "war on poverty" dollars never reach the poor at all . . . and how almost everyone in America is on welfare, except that it's called "farm subsidies" or "defense contracts" or "guaranteed loans" or "oil depletion allowances" or "tax-free capital gains"—in short, socialism for the rich and free enterprise for the poor. The book also details how President Nixon's so-called welfare reform bill, the "Family Assistance Plan," is not reform at all, but a sad step backward into the early 1960's.

America is at a crucial turning point. We can either "get tough," as a lot of politicians sloganeer—which means that we'll let children go hungry—or we can rekindle the American spirit of compassion for one another, and especially compassion for our children, by providing them with the essentials they need to grow to be self-supporting, responsible, productive citizens.

The choice we face as a nation, today, is more than just welfare reform. We must choose what kind of a people we want to be.

—Dr. George A. Wiley
Executive Director,
National Welfare Rights Organization

Acknowledgments

We would like to thank Bruce Thomas, Reverend Henry Mahaney, and Flora Seefeldt for the help they gave us in organizing the Milwaukee County Welfare Rights Organization.

Attorneys Richard M. Klein, Steven Steinglass, and James Scott provided us with much valuable legal aid.

The staff of the National Welfare Rights Organization, particularly Dr. George A. Wiley, James Evans, John Kaufman, and Peggy Winkler, have been of great help to us.

We thank Mary Lehman, Ellen Rigger, Ann McEvoy, Rita Gross, Diane Wirth, Jack Brown, Leo Barton, Ramona Angeles, Gerald and Cynthia Kretmar, and Edward O'Hara for the work they contributed in the preparation of this book. Also of great assistance were David Stanley Ford and Charles Lockwood. They all aided the book's editors, Reverend Dismas Becker and Thomas Howard Tarantino.

George Brockway of W. W. Norton & Company has been a kind friend.

Special thanks go to Georgia Griggs and Nancy Steffen for their help in the hard process of bringing this work to print.

Acknowledgments

Finally, we wish to thank the National Welfare Rights Organization Executive Board and all the members of the NWRO, without whom there would not have been a book.

—Mrs. Cassie B. Downer
Chairman, Milwaukee County
Welfare Rights Organization

Welfare Mothers Speak Out

We Ain't Gonna Shuffle Anymore

Laws do little good unless people know about them. For a poor person to hold rights in theory satisfies only the theory. We have to begin asserting those rights—and help the poor assert those rights. Unknown, unasserted rights are no rights at all.

—Nicholas deB. Katzenbach, as Attorney General of the United States, November 12, 1964

We're gonna lay down our shufflin' shoes
Down by the welfare door,
Down by the welfare door,
Down by the welfare door,
We're gonna lay down our shufflin' shoes
Down by the welfare door,
'Cause we ain't gonna shuffle anymore.

—Welfare Rights song

1. The Real Welfare Crisis

Everybody—well, almost everybody—in this country is on welfare, and everybody—well, almost everybody—hides it. In fact, most of America's welfare programs aren't even called "welfare," but, if they were, the line-up would be something like this:

Marriage Relief. Married couples file joint income tax returns, permitting them to pay less in individual taxes than single persons do. This program provided approximately $1.6 billion in benefits in the fiscal year 1970.

Aid to Families with Dependent Houses. This program allows homeowners to deduct the interest paid on their house mortgages from income for tax purposes, and it gave $2.6 billion to its beneficiaries in fiscal 1970. Unfortunately, no similar program exists for renters.

Aid to the Permanently and Totally in Debt. This program, which provided $1.7 billion in benefits in fiscal 1970, permits consumers to deduct all interest payments on credit purchases from their income before taxes are paid. Most people with charge accounts are taking advantage of this welfare program.

Aid to Dependent Students. In fiscal 1970, students received $60 million in scholarships and fellowships that were not counted as income. They also received $525 million in additional personal income tax exemptions, beyond those provided by the Personal Allowance System (the next program). Furthermore, students that year got government-supported loans saving them $225 million in interest payments. Students know that being old enough to vote makes them old enough to receive welfare.

Personal Allowance System. Everyone who earns money benefits from this basic welfare program, the personal income tax exemptions that allow each taxpayer to exclude $750 from taxable income for each of his dependents. The real value of this exemption, however, is not the present $750; it is the amount of tax that would have to be paid if the exemption did not exist. For a migrant farm worker earning $1,000 a year, the real value of this exemption is only $107.50. For a doctor or lawyer earning $100,000 a year, however, it amounts to $517.50. Thus the Personal Allowance System, which provided benefits of $25 billion in 1970, gives most of its aid to the rich, not to the poor. The majority of this country's other hidden welfare programs do the same.

Public Assistance to Charitable Donors. Those who contribute to charity can deduct their donations from their income taxes; the government clearly makes it most blessed to both give and receive. Such donors got $3.4 billion in benefits from this program during fiscal 1970.

Aid to Investors. This is a multifaceted program for those earning money from dividends, stock sales, life insurance savings, or investments. For income in the form dividends, the first $100 is not counted. Income derived from the sale of stock is subject to the capital gains exemption, which taxes only half of the earnings. Interest on life insurance savings is not included at all as income. Investors receive investment credits. In fiscal 1970, $11.5 billion was provided by this disguised welfare program.

Resource Exploiters' Assistance Program (REAP). Those who profit from the earth's natural resources are the beneficiaries of this generous and ingenious welfare program. Some farm income, timber company earnings, and coal and iron royalties are treated as capital gains and taxed at half the normal rate. This aspect of REAP provided more than $1 billion in benefits in fiscal 1970.

Another part of REAP is *Oil Producers' Public Assistance,* which permits income from oil to be taxed at lower rates than other income.[1] In fiscal 1970, it provided $1.5 billion in benefits to oil barons. Among them probably was Senator Russell Long of Louisiana, who collected $329,151 free from federal income tax between 1964 and 1969 because of this welfare program.[2] Senator Long, however, is adamantly opposed to welfare for the poor.

Still another part of REAP is the *Farm Subsidy Program,* which pays farmers not to plant crops. In other words, people reap what they are paid not to sow. One prominent beneficiary of this program—another anti-welfare-for-the-poor Senator—James Eastland, received about $160,000 for not planting cotton on his farm in Mississippi in 1970. A second recipient, rugged individualist John Wayne, named his Arizona cotton ranches "Red River," "Rio Bravo," and "El Dorado," after his movies, and with his partners collected $810,000 that year for leaving them alone.[3]

Eastland and Wayne, however, were only two of the 415 farm owners (major corporations, banks, and large landowners, that is—not small, poor farmers) who got over $100,000 each in subsidies from the Department of Agriculture in 1970: 5 per cent of the nation's farmers got 40 per cent of the farm subsidy money.[4] And 9 companies received over $1 million each for not doing anything. For a list of these companies, and their 1968, 1969, and 1970 subsidy payments, see Appendix A.

Then, in 1970, Congress placed a limit of $55,000 per

crop on agricultural subsidies. The result? Eastland, Wayne, and the others simply divided their farms into different businesses, and they and their associates received almost the same amount of money as they had the year before. And, in fiscal 1971, $5.4 billion in tax money is being spent on this welfare program.[5]

"The government's policy of paying the farmers to grow nothing sure is working good, because that's what most of us are eating."

Mrs. Jean Rablin
Milwaukee, Wisconsin

America's huge, disguised welfare system benefits the rich, not the poor. Three hundred and one people enjoy its full reward: in 1969, they made more than $200,000 each without paying a cent to the federal government in taxes. Among them were fifty-six very fortunate people who earned over $1 million, tax free.[6] A tip of our hat, though, goes to Governor Ronald Reagan of California, a millionaire who, in 1970, had a house provided by the state, drew over $44,000 in salary, but still paid no state income taxes at all.[7]

Beyond hidden welfare, however, are direct benefits to business and the rich. In 1970 and 1971, Congress has provided a $200-million-a-year subsidy to ship-builders, a $125 million loan guarantee to the Penn Central Railroad, and a $200 million cost override, together with a $250 million loan guarantee, to the Lockheed Aircraft Corporation.[8]

But that is not all. In 1971, President Nixon called for "relief" to get this country out of its economic slump.

Most of this "relief" goes to business; it is contained in the investment tax credit part of the Aid to Investors program, and provides $9 billion a year in benefits.[9]

In sum, the United States Government gives $60 to $70 billion a year in assistance to business and the rich.[10] For a brief list of the welfare programs that provide these benefits, see Appendix B.

"This country's had socialism for years, only it's been upside down. The rich have known for a long time that socialism's a good thing, but it's about time they started sharing it with the poor."

Mrs. Margaret Courchaine
Milwaukee, Wisconsin

Yet there are welfare programs that do help the less than rich, even though the beneficiaries are careful not to think of them as "welfare." Among the 43 million people in this country who get such payments are the 26.2 million recipients of old age, survivors, and disability insurance (social security), the 8.4 million recipients of state and local government retirement assistance, the 1 million people on the federal government's civil service retirement rosters, and the 2.1 million people on the unemployment rolls. Payments to these people amounted to $41 billion in 1969. In addition, 5.5 million people benefit from veterans' programs, whose expenditures were $8 billion in 1969.[11]

Most people, therefore, do not know what they are talking about when they talk about welfare. What they call "welfare" is Public Assistance, which is just one of the many welfare programs in this country, but it is welfare for poor people.

In 1966, 7.7 million people got benefits from Public Assistance. Of these, 2.1 million were aged (Old Age Assistance), 84,000 were blind (Aid to the Blind), 588,000 were disabled (Aid to the Permanently and Totally Disabled), 4.7 million were mothers and dependent children (Aid to Families with Dependent Children), and 700,000 were on General Assistance.

By December, 1970, however, 13.8 million people were enrolled in the Public Assistance welfare program. Of these, 2.1 million were aged, 81,000 were blind, 900,000 were disabled, 9.6 million—more than twice as many as in 1966—were mothers and dependent children, and 1.1 million were on General Assistance.

As the number of people receiving Public Assistance has risen, so have the costs. In 1966, total payments were $6.3 billion a year. By the end of 1970, they had reached $14.3 billion a year, also more than twice as much as before, but still almost nothing compared to the aid provided to business and the rich.

Yet it is the rise in the rolls and the cost of the Public Assistance welfare program, alone, that has everyone talking about a "welfare crisis." This increase has been going on for the last five years. Why? Because poor people who had been eligible for welfare for the last five, ten, and even twenty years, and were not getting it, finally started to assert their *right to welfare.*

Since 1966, when the National Welfare Rights Organization (NWRO) was founded, people have been working to urge all the poor who are eligible for aid to get it. The resulting rise in the welfare rolls has occurred primarily in the Aid to Families with Dependent Children (AFDC) Program, which accounts not only for nearly 70 per cent

Chart 1-1 Number of Public Assistance Recipients of Money Payments by Program, June and December of Each Year, 1936 to Date.

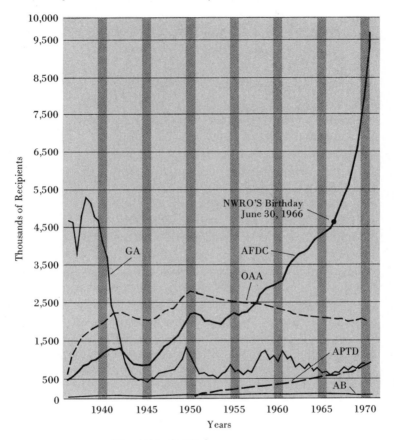

AB — Aid to the Blind
AFDC — Aid to Families with Dependent Children
APTD — Aid to the Permanently and Totally Disabled
GA — General Assistance
OAA — Old Age Assistance

of all the people on Public Assistance, but also for close to 80 per cent of all the new people joining the welfare rolls each month. NWRO, as Chart 1.A shows, has worked most with the mothers and children who are eligible for, or already on, AFDC.

If the welfare crisis in this country is the result of millions of poor people finally claiming benefits the law says they could have gotten long ago, then NWRO is one of the causes of it.

However, if the rising Public Assistance rolls is the welfare crisis, there should be a bigger one, because, as of December, 1970, the 13.8 million people receiving this type of welfare represent little more than half of those who are eligible for such benefits. States have acted to prevent 12 million poor people who could get aid from getting it. Yes, *almost* everybody in this country is on welfare.

The real welfare crisis, therefore, is not how many but how few poor people are receiving benefits. Now that the welfare system is finally being forced to deliver what it is supposed to under the law, everyone says there is a crisis, but the real crisis has been going on for a long time. It will continue until all the poor people in this country get their right to welfare.

2. Welfare Rights and the Welfare System

by Mrs. Mildred Calvert

Chairman, Northside Welfare Rights Organization
Secretary, Milwaukee County Welfare Rights Organization

When I first came on welfare, I was ashamed, because society has taught us to be ashamed of something like that. It's not something you go out and brag about, because you don't like to be degraded and humiliated. You already feel that way inside you because you are taught it from childhood. We were taught that welfare was begging, charity, and when you have a little pride, you don't want to do that. So, for a while, I hid it.

I heard about the Welfare Rights Organization through a cousin of mine. She kept trying to get me to go to these meetings with her and I said, "No, I'd never go to anything like that." But then I had a problem and I went to her with it and she kept telling me that she could take me to people who could help me and I still said "No." So I sat around and sat around and let the problem get out of hand, so finally I did go to the Welfare Rights people.

In the meantime, Milwaukee was having civil rights marches with Father James Groppi, and my kids were growing up and they were beginning to see that we were just as bad off as most of the people out there, so they told me that they were going on the marches for civil rights. Well, I was afraid of those kind of things. In fact, I was so brainwashed it was pathetic, but when the kids decided that they were going—the march came right by our house—I had to go with them. So, I went and followed Father Groppi.

I like to look at the news and read the newspaper. I've always loved to read, and I'd sit and I'd listen and I'd look. When I was reading *The Milwaukee Journal* and *The Milwaukee Sentinel* (the white newspapers), I read one story, when I was looking at the news on somebody's TV, I saw practically the same story, where we (the marchers) were doing all the bad things. I also noticed that when we went on the marches, we were the ones being fired upon with rocks and bricks and sticks, but it was as if we were doing the provoking when they put it on the news. So I started reading the black papers. I started reading things in a different light.

And I used to tell my children things weren't as bad as all that in the schools. But there were problems in all the schools and students were walking out and there was just problems all over. My children were getting so that they would just look at me kind of funny when they'd see me coming into the room, and if they were talking about certain things, they'd stop. I started looking into this and that, and I thought then that I would start talking to my children. That was when I started having rap sessions with them. Then I joined this organization.

Now I only joined Welfare Rights because of the problem I was having, not because I thought it was going to do me any good. I went and I heard them, and they were saying that this was bad and that was bad. I knew deep within that it was, but I was wondering how they could do anything about it. How could they do anything about something that's been that way for years and years? What could they do?

After I joined the organization, they took me and helped me settle the problem. They also found out that I'd never received any "special needs" (such as stoves and refrigerators, which can be obtained if the old ones break down) and stuff like that. Then I started getting interested in the meetings and listening to what these people were saying, and I realized that these people *were* doing something about a situation that has existed all these years but nobody before had ever thought enough of it to do anything about it.

Earlier, when I heard that they were going to unionize welfare in Welfare Rights groups, I thought, along with the rest of the people, that it was a disgrace to think that you're taking somebody else's money and using it and then forcing them to do things for you. Forming a union, how could it work? I couldn't see it.

That's when I learned of the welfare laws and the Supreme Court decisions and that welfare is a right and not a privilege, and I started wanting to learn more and more about it.

At first I was really bad. I just can't believe that all of a sudden I got to be a different person, but at the first, when the people from Welfare Rights were talking to me about my problem and were fighting for me at the Welfare Department, I was doing the same thing that I have had people do to me now. That is to say, "Well, my problem's not exactly quite that bad." You see, the Welfare Rights people had said that because of my having to spend this extra money and because of my having to do these extra things for my family, things that welfare wasn't giving to me when it should under the law, that I would run out of food. And I would, but I was too afraid to tell them. I was really afraid—I wasn't just bad—I was afraid.

I was afraid that the Welfare Department would say I was a bad mother and try to take my children from me, and I was afraid of being accused of neglect and fraud and stuff like that. Because I didn't know that I had a legal right to these things, you see. Until you become involved in Welfare Rights and really learn that welfare is your right, you'll be that way.

So when I started learning things better myself, I was really rapping with the kids because I was wanting them to teach me what they were finding out and why they were so upset—why they couldn't accept things today as I accepted them when I was coming along.

Little by little, I was beginning to realize what the kids were saying was true. They were saying things like the school system was bad, that they couldn't relate to it.

It finally dawned on me what my children meant, say about last year. I remember when I was a little girl, I lived in St. Louis. In St. Louis, we only had one river, and that was the muddy Mississippi. Right on the outskirts we had the Merrimac, but they both were brown and dirty-looking, looked like clay was all in them. I remember when I was in school when we'd draw the sky and the water together the teachers would have us make the water a deep blue, and they'd have us color the sky a lighter blue, so you could see the clouds and things in it.

I remember that I never believed it, I even read about it in geography books, but I never believed it because I didn't believe that water could be that color. I'd never seen it. Water was only white and pure-looking from the faucet, and brown in the river. That I could relate to, but I couldn't relate to the sky and water mixture being blue.

So that is why I can understand that my kids can only relate to what they can see.

Later on, I started thinking about other things that I used to think about when I was a kid, so I knew what my children were meaning when they were telling me things.

After that—it was the summer of 1969—I started learning about the Wisconsin welfare cuts coming. I found out through a caseworker after she found out that I belonged to Welfare Rights. She didn't tell me for a while, but then, just before she left the Welfare Department, she did.

So we went to the capital in Madison to protest the cuts. That's when I really started learning. I had been learning little by little, but that's when I really learned how bad the system is, how we are really hated, and how people could make you feel degraded and how humiliating it really is to be a welfare recipient to a person who just really doesn't understand. I sat there and listened to the legislators determining that we had taken over their assembly and that they would not listen to us and that they were going to call in the National Guard and this, that, and the other, and I had to cry. My children didn't understand why I was crying but, all of a sudden, I realized what we were up against, and then I was determined to fight. I was determined.

When we got back to Milwaukee, I heard about this organizer coming in. He was going to get the people organized and teach us how to organize—teach us how to keep ourselves together and teach us how to fight back. And that's what we're doing.

Now hear me good. Poor people have a right to welfare. Poor people have a right to life, not just to look forward to death and life after death, or to look forward to somebody coming down out of the sky and giving you a beautiful life later. We have a right to live decently as dignified human beings today.

When I see money being wasted—sending men to the moon to play golf, dumping nerve gas in the ocean, burning potatoes, killing off hogs, mutilating them, just getting rid of them—and then I see hungry and raggedy children running around, this is the kind of country that we live in, and this is what just burns me up. I feel the only way changes will be made, especially in the welfare system, is through poor people, welfare people, organizing and raising a lot of hell . . . which is all we can do.

3. Poverty Pimps

"We always have a lot of programs—poverty programs, Model Cities programs—and they all are geared around the poor. But nothing is actually filtered down to the poor. There are a lot of jobs created for other people, and when we do have an opportunity to participate in the jobs, we have the lowest-paying ones. Most of the jobs throughout the programs are no larger than a welfare check."

> Mrs. Johnnie Tillmon
> Los Angeles,
> Founding Chairman of the National
> Welfare Rights Organization and
> organizer of the country's oldest
> local Welfare Rights group

By now, everybody knows that if Mrs. Tillmon or Mrs. Calvert raise too much hell, they will be offered those low-paying jobs just to keep them quiet.[1] So who *really* benefits from the poverty program? The people who run it.

Since the birth of the Office of Economic Opportunity (OEO)—the country's antipoverty agency—in 1964, hundreds of corporations have found that they can get richer off poverty itself. To begin with, in the past seven years, about $600 million has gone to contracts for the study, evaluation, revision, and operation of the poverty program; 254 companies each have received $100,000 or more in OEO contracts, including 44 separate evaluations of Project Headstart.[2]

And many of these 254 private companies either were founded by former officials of the antipoverty agency or have employed its personnel. At the end of fiscal year 1970, OEO was paying on 128 consulting, evaluation, technical assistance, and support contracts worth $56,746,275. One out of every four of these was held by a group of 16 companies, which, all together, employed 35 former antipoverty officials. These 32 contracts were worth $11,507,978.[3]

There are countless examples of the movement of these antipoverty officials between OEO and private management and consulting firms. Among them: Gerson Green, who was Chief of Demonstration Projects for OEO until November, 1969, has been Director of Planning and Program Development for the University Research Corporation. As of June 30, 1970, this company, which was founded in 1965, held four antipoverty contracts worth $1,110,418. Robert Levine, who was a top executive in the RAND Corporation "think tank," worked briefly for OEO's Office of Research, Plans, Programs, and Evaluation. During that time, RAND received two contracts worth $600,000. When Mr. Levine resigned from the agency, he returned to RAND. Alfred Boerner, once on OEO's legal staff, went into private law practice where one of his clients was John D. Kettelle and Company, which has a $769,262 contract to evaluate OEO's Legal Services Program. Mr. Boerner briefly helped Kettelle administer the project. Bertrand Harding, who served as Deputy Director of OEO from 1966 to 1968 and was acting Director before Donald Rumsfeld took over, worked briefly for Fry Consultants, Incorporated, another OEO contractor, after he left the agency.[4]

Obviously, these intermovements are "improper," or so OEO has admitted. To stop them, and "extensive deficiencies in the review and monitoring of contracts and grants as well as widespread lack of proper management," then-OEO Director Rumsford called—in April, 1970—for new contracting regulations.[5] Such rules declared that no sole-source contract—a contract awarded without competitive bidding—could be granted to any company that employs in a senior position an individual who has worked for OEO within the year previous to the company's bid, unless a specific exemption is granted by the Director. The same rule was to apply to competitive contracts unless there was an exemption from the Deputy Director.

These regulations should have ended the improprieties. However, between April and November of 1970, at least four special exemptions were granted. One went to the Kettelle Company, which had employed Mr. Boerner, and the other three went to Abt Associates, Incorporated, which employed a former staff member from a regional office of OEO.[6]

The regulations had also demanded that each contractor disclose to OEO the names of former agency personnel he employs, the name of any agency employee with whom his company is negotiating for a job, and the name of any agency employee who holds, or whose family holds, a large interest in the private concern. As a result, in November, 1970, OEO revealed that fifty-eight former staff members were working for thirty-one companies that had bid on government contracts since the new regulations.

However, OEO refused to reveal the names of employees who were either negotiating with the companies for jobs or holding large financial interests in them.[7]

Volt Information Sciences, Incorporated, "a service organization engaged in all phases of man's communication with man," represents the classic case of a company using connections with OEO to make millions, so it will be dealt with in detail. Since 1965, this company has collected close to $30 million in poverty money.[8]

In the beginning, Volt established its office directly across the street from OEO headquarters and later was given floor space and desks inside the federal offices themselves, which is directly against government regulations. It then went to work on the government employees.[9] Jack Knapp, a Volt official, entertained them so lavishly that he was given the name "Credit Card Jack." William Kelly, the former Job Corps Director, was lured away from the government and now is Volt's Marketing Director.[10] He is only one of the company's seven former OEO staff members, but he is a particularly important one. After coming to the concern, he maintained close relations with his former assistant, C. Robert Lane, who became acting Director of VISTA (Volunteers In Service To America) until his replacement by Carol Khosrovi in September of 1970.[11]

This relationship proved very profitable. Whereas other companies had arranged for exemptions from the Rumsfeld regulations, Volt seems to have ignored such rules and, in June of 1970, obtained three contracts for the establishment of VISTA regional training centers. Volt's proposal for these contracts contained résumés of two VISTA employees who were still on the OEO payroll. Upon the signing of the contracts, one of them became a Volt training director.[12]

Poverty Pimps

Volt's ability to obtain OEO contracts is amazing, for the company has been strongly criticized by the anti-poverty agency for poor performance. Before the company was awarded the three VISTA training contracts, the head of the agency's Selection Division said that he had received complaints that Volt not only had done a bad job but had run up unnecessary overcharges.[13] Among these complaints was a 1969 review of Volt's performance on a "technical assistance" contract:

> Volt has not fully met the contract specifications for training and orienting specialists. Only a limited number of the training conferences which were contractually required have been conducted. . . . The contractor has failed to establish minimum training requirements for its specialists and has taken little initiative to obtain clarification from OEO. . . . By the end of the contract year, February 15, 1969, actual administrative costs will exceed original estimates by $310,000 to $340,000 or 80 percent to 90 percent. . . . Since Volt was awarded the . . . contract largely because it was the low bidder, the actual cost experience raises serious questions about the validity of Volt's initial cost estimates and OEO's acceptance of them.[14]

But one additional fact makes Volt's performance incredible. On March 30, 1970, Jack Shaffer, Director of the Office of Evaluation, submitted a report on VISTA training programs to C. Robert Lane. Mr. Shaffer saw the University of Colorado Training Program as most effective, noting that "All centers should have as part of their preparation of volunteers an attitude producing an approach that approximates that of the University of Colorado Training Center." The training contract of the University of Colorado, which came up for renewal in June, 1970, was one of those awarded to Volt.[15]

Indeed, VISTA really stands for Volunteers In Service

To Administrators. Leo Kramer was Associate Director of the Office of Selection and Training for VISTA until 1966, when he resigned. Eleven months later, he started Leo Kramer, Inc., a company that has collected $1,972,912 in nine antipoverty contracts, including seven from VISTA. Gary Price served with Mr. Kramer at VISTA and later became President of Policy Management Systems Incorporated, founded in 1966. It has collected $3,307,913 in contracts, several involving VISTA.[16]

Yet the big antipoverty money has been siphoned from the poor in programs dealing with jobs. The Job Corps, a billion-dollar program that supposedly gives poor teenagers training and jobs, has instead been just another source for new profits—in the "service" fields. What it has provided for the poor is not jobs but nebulous "employability" training.[17]

The Job Corps, however, has contributed some money to the poor; in 1966, for example, $6 million went directly to the families of needy enrollees. But that was nothing compared to its contributions to needy industrialists. In fiscal 1968 alone, they hauled off huge contracts:

> Litton Industries, for Camp Parks in California, $15.9 million; Federal Electric, a subsidiary of International Telephone and Telegraph, for Camp Kilmer in New Jersey, $10 million; Graflex Inc., a subsidiary of General Precision Equipment Inc., for Camp Breckinridge in Kentucky, $9.7 million; Burroughs Corporation, for the Omaha Job Corps center in Nebraska, $8 million; the Thiokol Chemical Corporation, for the Clearfield Center in Utah, $6.8 million; Philco, for the Tongue Point Center in Oregon, $6.3 million; and Westinghouse, for Camp Atterbury in Indiana, $6.3 million.[18]

One assumes that those companies did something to earn their money, but there are many others that get huge payments without doing any job training at all. Take a look at the JOBS (Job Opportunities in the Business Sector) program. Through June, 1970, nearly $500 million has been spent on it. Among its accomplishments have been the following:

One supermarket chain received a contract for $1.2 million to train 258 checkout workers. The contract provided for 47 weeks of on-the-job training; it was found that the checkout workers were able to take over their jobs on the first day, without any training at all.[19]

In another case, a $3.1 million contract, the government paid for a 30-week training course and workers received 20 minutes of training.[20]

Most outrageous is the fact that many employers simply use the JOBS program to subsidize their normal work force. The State Poultry Company in Jackson, Mississippi, for example, had 242 employees. It received a $408,190 contract to hire 140 JOBS trainees with wages beginning to $1.60 an hour and rising to $1.80.[21] Ninety per cent of another company's employees were JOBS trainees.

But when the "training" periods are over, most of the JOBS trainees lose their jobs. The retention rate across the country has varied from a low of 11.5 per cent in Seattle to a high of 49 per cent in San Francisco.[22]

"We feel we're just urban prostitutes. Anybody can draw up a proposal and present it to HEW and the health people and the OEO people and say they are going to do something for the poor, and make a lot of money off us."

Mrs. Johnnie Tillmon

Welfare Mothers Speak Out

Besides all the big-time poverty pimps, there are a lot of little ones. Among them are the social workers, many of whom are now more worried about professionalism, status, and money, than about poor people. One of the reasons state welfare costs are so high is that 10 to 20 per cent of all welfare expenditures go into bureaucracy —social workers, administrative superintendents, clerks, etc. It makes no sense to pay a person just out of college $8,000 a year to give almost nothing to a family of four . . . unless that person has his own hustle going.

"When I am traveling across the country, talking to many NWRO members, we discuss the fact that we are interested in the unemployment in this nation. We see that if an effort really was made to get rid of the welfare program, there would be a lot more unemployment than there is now. It seems that many people have nice, good-paying jobs because they are 'helping' us."

Mrs. Johnnie Tillmon

But too many welfare caseworkers are just helping themselves, not poor people. For example, in Milwaukee, it has been estimated that between seven and fifty Welfare Department social workers and employees are also landlords and collect rent from welfare recipients. At least four of these cases have been verified, despite the ease with which ownership can be hidden—by putting a corporate, partnership, or relative's name on the deed. These people are no fools; they use their knowledge of the Wisconsin welfare laws to charge the state's maximum amount for rent.[23] And there are no laws preventing them from making more than just their salaries off the poor.

Poverty Pimps

Finally, in any city in this country there are "arrangements" between Welfare Department personnel and small-time merchants. Take the case of an elderly Milwaukee woman who, unable to work because of a factory accident, applied to the Milwaukee County Welfare Department for General Relief. Her daughter and son-in-law, with whom she had been living, were moving, and thus she had to move, too. The apartment she found was unfurnished, but the only items she did not have were a stove, a refrigerator, and a kitchen table and chair. The Welfare Department issued a voucher for these items; it was sent to one of the used furniture stores in the city.

When the woman arrived at the store, the owner showed her the items he had selected for her. The refrigerator was pathetically small and badly scratched, the stove was not in much better shape, and the table was badly beaten up. The woman refused to buy the junk and went to several other stores. In one, she found that she could get a newer, larger refrigerator, a better stove, and a good table and chair for the same price as the voucher. When she asked her caseworker to transfer the voucher to the other store, she was told that the change could only be made by the Welfare Department's Business Office. When she called there she was told that the voucher would not be transferred and that she would have to get the items at the first store. The owner of the first furniture store had worked in the Business Office for eight years.

4. At War with the War on Poverty

by Mrs. Betty Niedzwiecki

Chairman, MOM's Welfare Rights Organization
Editor, Milwaukee County Welfare Rights Organization Newsletter

Before I came on welfare, I was working and getting divorced from my husband. Then I got in an accident at work, and my compensation ran out, and then I had a nervous breakdown. The compensation only ran for eighteen to nineteen weeks and then I was out of luck. The breakdown was from too much pressure from too many people.

I went on welfare so I could stay home with the kids because they were getting completely out of control. The baby was three at the time, and he had never really been with me. I had been working since he was born. He couldn't even associate with me, and I just couldn't take that anymore. I decided that until my kids are old enough to realize what work is all about, the government owes it to me to bring up my children. The government owes me because I am raising two boys that I am sure they'll be taking into their armed services one of these days to fight their damn wars.

Now I am getting $109 a month plus rent for myself

and two children. I should get a lot more than that. I should get paid at least $15 a day, per child, for taking care of my children, because that's what the Welfare Department pays when it has to send a homemaker in if a mother on welfare is in the hospital.

The Milwaukee County Zoo feeds the monkeys on 33 cents a meal, but Milwaukee County gives the monkeys on welfare only 16 cents a meal. I guess if you live in a better neighborhood—the Zoo is in the suburbs—you get more money. That's how they think of us: we're not human beings, we're just animals.

When I went on welfare, they stuck me in an experimental zone. The caseworkers in there were working for the people as much as they possibly could. They even belonged to Milwaukee's Friends of Welfare Rights. They told me about Welfare Rights in the first place. They informed me of a lot of things that go on. It's not that they weren't allowed to do it, either. It wouldn't get them into any trouble to tell me what they told me. But the Welfare Department just closed down the zone.

In fact, they recently changed around all the offices in the Welfare Department. They say they did it for convenience, but they did it because Welfare Rights learned where the supervisors' offices were and how to get to them. They got tired of us walking in and yelling at them and demanding our rights.

One of the supervisors at the Department once told me, "If it was left up to the majority of the social workers in the building, recipients would get much bigger checks, and would get everything they needed. There is one easy way to do it. The majority of us should just get up and walk out and strike for poor people. Get out in the streets and get a picket line going with ourselves and the poor people. And say that we want to be able to give better service to the people or we don't want to be giving service at all. It would be beautiful, but we'd all be fired and we wouldn't have a job." I said to him, "Well, you just told me that you don't want a job that you can't do nothing for people with, anyway!"

The Welfare Department should be turned over to people who know how to handle problems. It should be set up so that when a person comes in, it should have his case opened and him out of there in an hour and a half. No more of this ninety-two copies of everything: that's a bunch of bull. Nobody reads reports that are sent to Washington anyhow. It's all put in a file drawer. Unless someone decides to investigate it, maybe six or seven years later. Yeah, six or seven years later, when right now a mother is standing there with five kids who haven't got anything to eat and it takes them a month to open the case.

There are cops at the Welfare Department. They say they're there in case someone starts some real trouble, but they're so busy following Welfare Rights people that if the food stamp department got held up, they'd be nowhere around. I go in there, say, on the 5th and the 20th of the month (welfare check days), which are the busiest days for food stamps, and immediately the cops will start following me and leave all the people standing in the food stamp line—hundreds of people. When I'm up on the second floor, the cops are right there with me, but food stamps are on the first.

The sheriffs talk a lot about law and order. But they cause more trouble than they're worth. I would be there yelling at a caseworker because he won't give a woman $100 for a washing machine—he'll only give her $75. Well, the law says she can get $100, but who are the cops after? Me, not the caseworker.

And the law says people must be given aid within

thirty days from when they apply, but they never get it, and the cops don't arrest the Welfare Department. They aren't going to bite the hand that feeds them.

And they don't work too hard, either, because you don't need much to tell poor people to shut up, and get out, and stop raising that ruckus because you didn't get your check three or four days ago when you should have and your kids are starving.

The Welfare Department's not the only thing that's a lot of bull. All the poverty programs are bull. Like VISTA Volunteers. They're people who get out of college with nothing to do, they've been taken care of all their lives by their mothers and fathers and sheltered from the ways of the world. So when they get their college diploma, someone hands them a pamphlet saying, "You don't know what to do with your life right now, so be a VISTA Volunteer and help the poor people." And they think they're going to go out and do a great big beautiful job.

So they join VISTA. They don't know what to do anyhow when they get there, but even if they did, it wouldn't do them any good, because they're put in some situation where they can't do anything anyway, because the government doesn't really want to help poor people; it just wants it to look like it's trying.

Now the government said that we have to have some kind of poverty program in the United States because poor people are just getting worse and worse and nobody's helping them. So they took a nice big bunch of money and stuck it into all these poverty programs. Third Street in Milwaukee might as well be called "Agency Row" because there are so many government-funded programs there, and they aren't doing anything, even for the people that live in the immediate area. I live a couple of blocks from Third Street and there's never been a worker on this block contacting people, so you know they don't do anything for the rest of the city. Nobody ever does anything. But they all get paid from $5,000 to $12,000 a year from OEO because the federal government said we've got to have a poverty program.

In Milwaukee, the basic agency is the Inner City Development Project (ICDP). Now the ICDP's are so bad that they don't even give recipients bus tickets to the Welfare Department when they have to go because it's check day and their checks didn't come. Welfare recipients are supposed to get the bus tickets needed to get to the Welfare Department from the social worker at the Welfare Department.

Let me tell you a story about one guy who works at an ICDP center. He was talking to a friend of mine one night and said, "Boy, did I have a busy day, I referred eleven people." My friend said, "Okay, but what'd you do for them?" He said, "Man, I referred 'em, I referred 'em."

But it's the Medical Assistance Program that's the worst. My mother's been crippled since I was five years old, and I don't remember ever seeing her out of a wheelchair. We tried all these charitable foundations—they've been doing hip surgery for ten, twelve years—but every time we inquired they said we would have to pay half the cost. We couldn't afford that.

I said we should try the Medical Assistance Program, but my mother said she'd tried there for a long time and always failed. I told her, "Look, you don't have any money, you should be able to get the operation done here in Milwaukee on the medical card." It was a fight to get her the Title 19 card, though, because the Medical Assistance place just plain lied.

People go down to get a Title 19 card and anybody who's not on welfare gets a Group 2 card automatically, which doesn't cover anything. It will cover your eye examination, but it won't cover the cost of glasses. So why bother to get your eyes examined if you ain't got the cash to buy the glasses, right?

Like I say, my mother had been trying for years to get a Medical Group 1 card to cover the operation. I went down by myself to find out what the requirements were to be able to get a Group 1 card. You had to either be on AFDC or on General Relief, and then it covered just the children, or you had to have an income of less than $800 a year—that's what they told me. I said, "That just doesn't sound right. The government usually does it in five hundreds—$500, $1,000, $1,500; it doesn't fool around with $800 a year."

With the help of Welfare Rights people, I found out that it was $1,500 a year. So we sent the Medical Assistance place a letter telling them that they would be liable for a suit, because they kept my mother from having medical attention all this time when she's in very bad need of it, unless they sent the medical card immediately. My mother got the card four days later.

To sum it all up, they ought to take all the money wasted in these poverty programs and divide it among the poor people. They'd be doing a lot more to end poverty than they're doing now.

5. Welfare Fraud

But, Mrs. Niedzwiecki, it is "welfare" that has been set up to provide the money to combat poverty, and this country's Public Assistance system is dominated by the program you're in, Aid to Families with Dependent Children (AFDC).

"What's 'welfare'? Welfare's when the government passes a law to give aid to the poor and then tries to keep the poor from getting it. Now I don't like to use the word welfare because, according to Noah Webster, welfare means health, happiness, and comfort, and I haven't had any of that for the six years that I've been on AFDC."

Mrs. Johnnie Tillmon

Here is the way that AFDC is supposed to work. Under the federal AFDC laws and regulations, each state must provide assistance to those who qualify and must grant a fair hearing to any individual whose application for aid is to be denied or whose application will not be acted upon with reasonable promptness (thirty days). There are privacy safeguards designed to protect the rights of welfare applicants, ensuring that they disclose only information directly concerned with their eligibility for aid. Local, durational residency requirements for assistance are outlawed, a ruling that gives the poor the same right as anyone else to move around the country.

AFDC serves mothers and their dependent children. If the mother remarries, like most women receiving child support, she does not burden her new husband, for she continues to receive state support for her dependent children, unless her new husband adopts them. Also, the presence in her house of a man who is not included in the welfare grant does not necessarily make her family ineligible for aid.

The determination of a family's eligibility for welfare and the computation of its monthly grant appears to be done in a reasonable way. The earnings of a dependent child in school are not included as income. Neither the first $30 of a mother's monthly income nor one-third of the remainder is counted. This encourages the AFDC family to work. There is a guard against those who would voluntarily limit their work time, too, for such persons would lose the "$30-plus-a-third" exemption. Also, food stamps and payments for relocation forced by highway expansion are not included as income.

Each state is to set up a Work Incentive (WIN) Program, and all appropriate recipients must be referred to it. A training incentive, money that is also not counted as income, is provided for them, but they are to be cut out of the welfare grant if, without good reason, they refuse to accept employment. However, notice of a cut must be given to any recipient, and the recipient can demand—and get—a fair hearing before he or she is actually cut.

The federal AFDC law makes family services available. These assist recipients toward self-support, a stronger family life, and child development. Family planning must

be offered to recipients wishing it; this includes everything from information to contraceptives. Each state must
have a program to prevent or reduce out-of-wedlock
births and is entitled to try to find paternity and secure
support from the father of any such born child. Child-care
services are available to all people participating in the
Work Incentive Program. States also can appoint "protec-
tive payees" to protect children from a relatives' misuse of
their welfare payments. And basic medical services are
provided to all recipients.[1]

Each state is allowed to adopt its own system to put
the national program into effect, but the states must obey
the federal laws and regulations. The importance of this
can be seen in the crucial part of the AFDC program, the
amount of money provided recipients. Each state may set
its own level of payment. However, one section of the
federal law demanded that by mid-1969

> . . . the amounts used by the State to determine the needs
> of individuals will have been adjusted to reflect fully changes
> in living costs since such amounts were established, and
> any maximums that the State imposes on the amount of aid
> paid to families will have been proportionately adjusted. [42
> USC 602 (a) (23)]

Now all of this sounds fair, and those who don't have
to live on AFDC may even think it a humane system, but
in practice it is an insult to human dignity and justice.

And the most notable example of AFDC's injustice con-
cerns the provision for a cost-of-living increase. The law
seems to require states to increase both "the amounts used
to determine the needs of individuals" and the maximums
imposed "on the amount of aid paid." Across the country, these payment maximums have limited the amount
provided AFDC families depending upon the number of

children in the grant. The maximum in a state, for example, may be $94 a month for a mother and one child, $119 a month for a mother and two children, and so on.

The Department of Health, Education, and Welfare (HEW), however, twisted words to void the effects of the law. First, it created two new welfare indices; they are here called the *standard of need* ("the amounts used to determine the need of individuals") and the *standard of payment* ("the amount of aid paid"). Then, it said that states had to raise the standard of need, but not necessarily the standard of payment. Why? Because the order to raise the standard of payment was to apply only to the states that had absolute maximum grants. One state with such grants is Maryland, with a ceiling of $250 a month on all welfare grants. This means, for example, that a family of six and a family of ten would receive the same monthly assistance.

HEW's distortion of the cost-of-living-increase requirement freed states to raise the standard of need and, at the same time, cut actual payments to recipients. This many states did. They also cut "special" grants for recipients having diabetes, asthma, and other ailments. The cheated poor responded with anger and violence; in Wisconsin, for one, welfare mothers seized the State Assembly.

But this injustice was exposed in the case of Mrs. Ruth Jefferson of Dallas, Texas. The AFDC grant for her and her five children—$135 a month—had been cut by nearly 10 per cent in September, 1968. The next May, their grant was cut again under the formula that raised the Texas standard of need and then paid only 50 per cent of it. Mrs. Jefferson sued. She charged the State Welfare Agency with failing to raise AFDC payments as demanded by federal law. On July 1, 1970, a three-judge Federal Court in Dallas found that Texas, in cutting its welfare grants, had violated the law and ordered the state to increase AFDC payments to reflect an 11 per cent increase in the cost of living. In its decision, the Court attacked HEW's interpretation of the law:

> Texas and HEW . . . argue, in effect that the statute is not a command to pay more, but a command to make a bookkeeping entry regarding cost of living increases which would instantly be nullified by the payment of a lesser percentage of the book entry. This is a cipher game. We are of the opinion that Congress intended no such academic exercise. We believe instead that Congress desired to increase the size of grants actually reaching AFDC recipients so as to minimize the effect of the rise in the cost of living. Such an interpretation is more consistent with both the language of the statute and with common sense. . . . We are also convinced that Congress did not see Section 402 (a) (23) (codified as 42 USC 602 (a) (23)) as a mirage, but rather signaled a hope that children would be granted the fact of an increased payment and not the fiction of an increased standard. [*Jefferson* v. *Hackney*, 304 F. Supp. 1332]

In the end, however, common sense was ruled out and fiction ruled in; in 1970, the Supreme Court declared in *Rosado* v. *Wyman* (397 U.S. 397) that the cost-of-living provision did not demand an increase in the amounts actually paid to AFDC recipients.

Yet cost-of-living-increase decreases are not the only destructive ploys used by states against the poor. Worse are the tricks states play to prevent people from even getting on welfare in the first place.

There should be no residency requirements as a condition of aid, but for years, forty-one states required newcomers to wait for one year before they could qualify for welfare. In 1969, the Supreme Court ruled that these laws were an unconstitutional discrimination against newly arrived people and an infringement on their right to travel. Using them, state governments had prevented all too many mothers and children from receiving assistance.

The Supreme Court ruling did not stop the illegal state requirements, though. As of April, 1970, six states still had them. And, early in 1971, two others, New York and Connecticut, passed new ones.

It is in their first contact with Welfare Departments, then, that most poor people are denied their rights. States must act within thirty days on a person's application for welfare and must provide a fair hearing to those who are to be denied it. Yet Welfare Department practice makes a mockery of the federal law:

More than 3,000 people in St. Louis, Missouri, were kept on a "waiting list" for months during 1970, and Missouri officials admitted that they were breaking the law.

The Sutter County, California, Welfare Department has devised a procedure for applicants in which they are courteously referred from the AFDC caseworker to the County General Relief worker to the Job Coordinator to the AFDC caseworker . . . each person explaining that he lacks the authority to deal with the applicant's particular case.[2]

A Puerto Rican family applied for welfare in New York City and were rejected. They managed to subsist through handouts of food and money and odd jobs that the father got temporarily. They moved from place to place, staying wherever a building superintendent would permit them. After three months, they met a lawyer who informed them that they *were* eligible for assistance, so they went back to the Welfare Department, where they were told that the Department had wrongfully denied them aid earlier. However, the Department wondered how, if the family was so destitute, they had managed to survive for three months. It said they must have some hidden income and rejected them again.

Finally, many states have used the federal AFDC law's "$30-plus-a-third" income exemption for working welfare recipients in a way that prevents low-wage-earners from getting on welfare. This exemption is used only for those already on aid, not for those with the same wages who are applying for it. Thus a mother with one child who works as a dishwasher or waitress may earn too much to get on welfare, but, if she were already on, she could have the same job with the same income and stay on.

"We know there are a lot of programs on the books. If they were implemented as they are supposed to be, people wouldn't suffer like they are suffering now."

Mr. Ramon Rodriguez
Immokalei, Florida

It is a combination of these illegal state and Welfare Department actions along with the total absence of published information about the right to welfare—after all, how many people know how much their state's welfare grants are?—that has enabled the states to deny welfare benefits to 12 million poor people in this country.

But these abuses are not occasional; they happen all over America. As of April, 1970, forty-nine out of the fifty states were operating their welfare programs in ways that violate the federal welfare laws and regulations. There are three ways in which a state can break these laws, ranging from outright defiance to subtle manipulation. First, a state can simply not bother to develop a federally approved plan. Second, a state can draw up an approved plan and add illegal amendments to it. Third, it can have an approved plan but never put it into practice. As of 1970, there were more than 500 such violations.

Many of these concern the AFDC cost-of-living-increase provision already discussed. This provision is the most important of all the laws because it directly affects the size of the welfare grant received by the millions of people on aid. Again, the states and HEW reacted to that law by inventing the indices of standard of need and standard of payment.

To begin with, the states' standards of need are inhumanly low. In Mississippi, for one, the standard is $232 a month for a family of four—any family of four needs more than that to live. In Maryland, for another, it is $302 a month, or $3,624 a year for a family of four. Maryland is a perfect example of the cipher game, for its standard of payment is only 65 per cent of need. Mississippi is even worse, for, while its standard of payment may also be $232, it only pays $70. The states and HEW have turned the cost-of-living provision into an empty moral platitude:

> [The] purpose of [the] provision . . . requiring states to adjust amounts used to determine needs to reflect change in living costs and to proportionately adjust the maximum AFDC paid is to require states to face up realistically to [the] magnitude of [the] public assistance requirement and lay bare the extent to which their programs fall short of fulfilling actual need and to prod states to apportion their payments on a more equitable basis. [*Rosado* v. *Wyman*, N.Y. 1970, 90 S. Ct. 1207, 397 U.S. 397]

So the states get away with a legal subterfuge by manipulating the two new welfare indices. However, twenty states even use the subterfuge illegally. Furthermore, like

Maryland, twenty-one states have arranged their standards in such a way as to be able to say to applicants for welfare, "Yes, you are eligible for welfare, but you are not eligible for any money." Finally, nineteen states, including Mississippi, do not even pay the full standard of payment, enabling them to say to welfare recipients, "You are entitled to more money than you are getting, but we are not going to give it to you." For a state-by-state comparison of standards of need and payment and actual payment levels, see Appendix C.

But the cost-of-living-increase requirement is only one of fifty-four federal welfare laws and regulations that were being broken by the states in 1970. Seven states were still trying to force a remarried welfare mother's new husband to assume support of her AFDC children. Eight states lacked proper fair-hearing procedures. And twelve states had infractions of the welfare eligibility regulations. These are not merely administrative laws and regulations, but devices that constantly deny millions of poor people billions of dollars of the assistance to which they are legally entitled. For a full list of these violations, see Appendix D.

Two recent incidents highlight the complete disregard that states have for both the federal welfare laws and regulations and the rights of the poor. The first occurred in Nevada in January of 1971, and it made front-page news; it was a massive cut in the welfare rolls. Of the entire caseload, 22 per cent were eliminated and another 29 per cent received reduced benefits. What didn't make the front page was the fact that the state "ran roughshod over the constitutional rights" of welfare recipients (according to a United States District Court ruling in March, 1971). The state of Nevada had also violated the federal law that demanded that an adequate notice of termination be given to recipients and that they be informed of their right to a hearing before being cut. The Court ordered Nevada not only to reinstate the people illegally cut from the welfare rolls, but also to make retroactive payments covering the time they had been off welfare.[3]

It is, however, California and its Governor, Ronald Reagan, who epitomize the states' lawlessness. Governor Reagan is the man who has said, "Welfare is a national moral and administrative disaster—a cancer that is destroying those it should succor. . . . And it threatens the security of those whose labor and generosity subsidizes the cheats and frauds."[4] Yet it is the Governor, himself, who has done the lion's share of cheating in his efforts to destroy those whom the welfare system should succor. In October, 1970, the Department of Health, Education and Welfare, after an earlier hearing, ruled that the state of California was breaking so many federal welfare laws and regulations—including the cost-of-living provision— that, if it didn't stop, it would lose the $684 million in federal contributions it was receiving. Such a cut-off is the main power that HEW has to enforce the federal welfare laws. By April, 1971, California still had not changed its welfare program to abide by the federal laws, but federal funds had not been cut off because Reagan had maneuvered with President Nixon to prevent it.[5]

California, however, is not the only state to come close to losing federal contributions to its welfare programs. Indiana, Nebraska, and Connecticut are others whose many violations have provoked similar threats.

"This is a country where one of our children goes out and steals $70 and the government makes him spend twelve years in jail and then kills him when he tries to escape. But the

same government forces people like him to steal in order to live because it cheats them out of billions in welfare benefits, and no one shoots the government. So what does 'law and order' really mean? It means that the biggest welfare fraud is the welfare system."

Mrs. Olivia Hazelwood
Milwaukee, Wisconsin

And welfare fraud is even more pervasive in the Medical Assistance Program. As of April 1, 1970, twenty-one states did not have legally acceptable methods for preventing doctors from charging excessive rates for Medical Assistance. Nineteen states did not have plans to force doctors to keep proper records of their medical services available for state audit. Twenty-two states did not guarantee individuals eligible for medical assistance a free choice as to who provides those services. Twenty-one states did not have acceptable standards for skilled nursing homes and hospitals, and twenty-five did not even have proper medical reviews of these institutions.

Is it any wonder, then, that doctors commit welfare fraud? In 1968, about 11,000 doctors each received $25,000 or more in Medical Assistance payments. There appeared to be so many cases where such income was not reported for taxes that a detailed Internal Revenue Service tax audit on a sample of 4,000 returns was begun. By September, 1970, preliminary results were in on 3,000 of the 4,000. They showed that about 50 per cent of the 3,000 doctors' tax statements had "substantial deficiencies" in the amount of income reported for taxes compared to the amount of income actually made. One doctor earned $158,591 over a three-year period, but reported only $18,590 of it.[6]

He, and those other doctors, must know that everybody benefits from welfare—except the poor. It is the *victims* of the welfare system, then—poor people—who must learn and demand their welfare rights.*

---

* To aid in this, a Bill of Welfare Rights is included in Appendix E.

6. The Welfare System Is an Indian-Giver

by Mrs. Loretta Domencich

Indian Organizer, Oh Gweh Oh (The Real People)
Welfare Rights Organization, Milwaukee, Wisconsin

When I was growing up, I always had the idea—and I don't remember anyone specifically giving it to me—that Indians were too proud to accept welfare and that therefore we really didn't have a lot of welfare recipients in the Indian community. We were a poor community, but we were too proud to accept welfare. Later, I realized that we had a lot of welfare recipients, because when we set up an American Indian Information and Action Center, recipients were mainly the ones that were coming in.

The whole thing just blew my mind: the fact that I had grown up with this lie my whole life and never questioned it, and the fact that there were people all around who were saying the same thing. Not only were other people thinking Indians weren't on welfare, but the Indian community was, too, because I was part of the Indian community that had believed for a long time that we didn't have any welfare recipients.

The Indians who were on welfare were suffering very much because our own people were saying, "If you're on welfare, then you must not be too proud." It was generally accepted that Indians who are proud don't go on welfare. The pride of the Indian is a really important thing. Now I think it's about time the Indian himself starts defining what being proud is and not depend on white society to define it for him.

I think Welfare Rights has also given me a clearer idea of racism. The Welfare Department has a way of lumping people together; whether you're black, white, red, or brown, you're all a bunch of niggers when you go into the Welfare Department.

The dignity of the welfare recipient caught me as an Indian idea. The dignity of the individual says that no matter what a person's capabilities are, whether he is the leader or whether he is a person who is crippled or elderly or can't do anything, he still has a place in the tribe. Welfare Rights is an Indian organization to me because I think a lot of things that Welfare Rights is going after are Indian ideas—Guaranteed Adequate Income is really an Indian concept. It is the way the Indians themselves ran their early communities.

So by the time I started organizing, one of the things I realized was that there were many, many Indians on welfare. There were some places, like in the Patowatomi tribe, where as many as 75 per cent of the people were getting some sort of public assistance. In Menominee County, where I finally decided to try to organize the first Indian Welfare Rights group in Wisconsin, about 60 per cent of the Menominee Indian population was receiving some kind of welfare.

Menominee County is a good example of the way that the welfare system treats all people who are on welfare, so let me tell you about it. In Menominee County, there had been a reservation set up under a treaty which gave the Indians the land as long as the grass is green and the sun shines and the rivers flow. But in 1887, the Dawes Act was passed; it gave plots of land to individual Indians rather than allow the Indians to own their land communally as they had always done.

The Indians didn't understand the whole concept of ownership certificates and individual ownership—it seemed senseless for one individual to own a little piece of land and then keep the whole community out when you have to live in the community and are part of the community. It wasn't the idea that people could come from outside the community, cut all kinds of timber, and then leave. It was the idea that if the person came in and made himself a part of the community, he could use whatever the rest of the community had, and that included land.

The Menominee Indians were the only tribe in Wisconsin that was really together at that time and ignored the Dawes Act, kept their reservation intact, ignored the allotment of land to individuals, and kept their land in trust to the tribe.

When the reservation was terminated in 1961, they still had their complete reservation, whereas most of the other reservations in Wisconsin are all cut up; they're just little patches of land all over. The Menominees had money in the bank, they ran their own hospital, they had their own social services and took care of their own welfare recipients. They had their own school system and took care of their own street repair. They were a little community that was sufficient unto itself. They had their lumber mill, which was the basis of the whole economy. Why, then, was the reservation terminated?

Well, the Menominees had put in a suit against the federal government for mismanagement of their timber rights. Since they were a reservation, their land and all their holdings were kept in trust by the Bureau of Indian Affairs. Whenever they cut any timber, they had to go through the Bureau. The Bureau also had to okay any contracts that the Menominees made as far as having the timber cut. Everything went through the Bureau. It had to make some kind of judgment on any business that went on on the reservation. Several years before termination, the Menominees found out that the Bureau was mismanaging the money that was made from the cutting of the timber on the reservation. They put in a lawsuit against the Bureau of Indian Affairs, and in 1951 they won an $8.5 million judgment.

Immediately after they won the suit, the federal government started talking about the fact that the Menominee Indian Reservation was now ready to be terminated, for they were now ready to be self-sufficient and to get out from under the wing of the federal government and the Bureau of Indian Affairs. The Menominees were completely against this. But the federal government had this money—the $8.5 million—and they held it over the Menominee Indians' heads. Unless the Menominees terminated, they were not going to get the money.

This whole coercion was strictly illegal, the old story of people being oppressed because their oppressor doesn't give them a complete understanding of what the situation is. The Menominees didn't realize that the senators were lying to them and using coercion; they believed that they were not going to get that money unless they signed the termination bill.

After the reservation was terminated, a corporation of Menominee Indian stockholders was set up and each Menominee received 100 shares of stock in Menominee Enterprises, Incorporated. It owned the land and the mill and all the economic interests in newly created Menominee County. It ran all the businesses for the stockholders, but, without consulting the Menominees, a trust was set up for all indigents and all minors.

Any person on welfare of any kind was not considered capable of handling his own affairs, which is ridiculous. Welfare recipients are in such a tight economic situation that they have to be able to run their affairs even better than a person who is making $10,000 or $12,000 a year. Therefore, to say that a welfare recipient can't handle his own affairs is just not to understand the situation of the welfare recipient in the first place.

Anyway, all welfare recipients' stocks were put into this trust and they've never been able to vote in the corporation. What has happened is that welfare recipients can vote for anything else—President, senators, legislators, they can even vote for their county officials—but they can't vote in their own corporation.

Since termination in 1961, the bank which held the stocks in trust—the First Wisconsin Trust—has used the votes of welfare recipients and children. Parents were not even considered capable of voting for their own children. From the beginning, then, the bank controlled who was elected to the Menominee Enterprises Voting Trust which selected the Board of Directors. There are Menominees living all over the country, and the bank had 44 per cent of all of their votes, not just the ones in Menominee County.

It was pretty difficult to counteract the bank's 44 per cent when you had to get people from all around the country to fight what the bank could do in one vote. Gradually, more and more people didn't even bother to go to the annual corporation meetings. They knew that there was no way that they could defeat the bank, so people just became disinterested. You see, the bank has a long record of voting with the minority of Menominees even though it says it doesn't vote.

When the reservation was terminated, all the Menominees also were given bonds. The welfare recipients' bonds were automatically put into the First Wisconsin Trust, and then in 1964, when they got state social assistance into Menominee County, the state of Wisconsin passed a bill that specifically referred to Menominee Enterprise bonds, saying that whenever people went on welfare or were on welfare they had to assign their bonds to the state of Wisconsin. So when Menominees apply for welfare, they have to give up the bonds.

Welfare recipients can still collect interest on the bonds, though. The face value of each person's bond is $3,000, and it collects 4 per cent interest each year. For a full bond valued at $3,000, a welfare recipient could collect $120 a year, except for the fact that the bond is held by the bank, so it is never more than $100 because of the administrative cost charges. And when a welfare recipient got his check for about $100 each December, the Menominee Welfare Department used to subtract $100 from the welfare check. The first thing that we were able to do was to get the state of Wisconsin to consider the interest on the bond as inconsequential income and not take it back.

But the Menominee Enterprises bond itself is worthless. It was given to the Menominees in lieu of land. All the land is really owned by Menominee Enterprises, which gives each Indian a bond, so, supposedly, if he wanted to buy Menominee Couny land he could use his Menominee bond. However, you can't go to a bank, you can't even go to Menominee Enterprises and get any money on this bond; you can't sell it to anyone because, in this day of inflation and rising prices, no bank wants to be bothered with a bond that only collects 4 per cent interest, which is about half of what it could get on any other bond. The bond doesn't mature until the year 2000, so no bank wants to go through the paper work of buying it. Maybe a bank would buy the bond for a few hundred dollars, but that's about all a person can get for it.

The bonds aren't worth enough to keep a person off welfare. They should be considered inconsequential income because they have no market value. The only reason they cannot be considered inconsequential is because of the law that the state of Wisconsin passed in 1964. There already is legislation for other welfare recipients that says bonds don't have to be sold if selling them would mean taking an unreasonable loss, and that definitely is the case with the Menominee Enterprises Bond. The law discriminates against the Menominees, and then the state of Wisconsin says, "Sorry, we have a law which says we have to take the assignment of the bonds."

And the state has set up an arbitrary $1,800 value on the worth of the bond, but no bond has ever been sold for more than $1,200. The only time a person can actually get money for the bond is when he dies, and then Menominee Enterprises will buy the bond, if it is the person's only asset, for $1,200. But a living, breathing person cannot get close to that.

The state doesn't actually own welfare recipients' bonds. They just assign the bond to the state so if the holder dies or goes off welfare the state is supposed to take any welfare received off from the bond and then send the rest of it back to the recipient. But this has never happened. People have been on welfare for a few months, assigned their bonds to the state, then gone off welfare, and never received their bond back, or any part of it, and the state won't even give out information about what's happened to it.

But I can tell you what's happened to the Menominee Indians who are on welfare: the federal government originally took their land and gave them the reservation forever, took the reservation back, and gave them stocks and bonds, but the Menominees never saw the stocks and can't even vote with them, and they have to give up the bonds, which are worthless anyway while the Menominees are alive, in order to get welfare, and if they get off welfare they don't get the bonds back, even though the state is supposed to return them. Indian giving— that's what's happened to the Menominees.

But the welfare system is an Indian giver to everybody. It gives a little bit but it takes a whole lot out of an individual. An Indian giver is a person who gives you something one day, then takes it back the next. It may not be exactly the same thing, but he takes something more valuable in return. Long ago, white people coined the term "Indian-giver" when they saw what their fellows were doing to the Indians and couldn't—or wouldn't —do anything about it. Nothing's changed.

I think the whole welfare system is an Indian-giver because what it's doing is giving a little bit of money to individuals in order to keep them from dying right away, but what it's taking from them is their dignity, their self-determination, their morale, and any type of power. And we're going to get those things back.

7. Spanish-Speaking People and the Welfare System

by Mrs. Clementina Castro

Vice-Chairman, Union Benefica Hispana Welfare Rights Organization
Sergeant-at-Arms, Milwaukee County Welfare Rights Organization

Me and my husband and our three children came to Milwaukee. We were migrant workers. We were looking for better jobs either in the factories or in the fields. When I say fields, I mean picking tomatoes and all kind of things . . . working on a farm. We came here to have a better living. We thought, "He can work and I can work and our children can work no matter what their age," because in farm work you can be just seven years old.

It is very, very hard when you don't have the education to get a job, especially when you been working all the time on the farm and you can't go to the city and talk to the people. You don't know where to go, what direction to take, what kind of job you can get. It's very hard to find a new job and get used to it because all the time you been working in the fields. You come home tired and that's it.

If you come to the city and get on welfare, you feel that you are doing nothing—just waiting for the money. We can't sit around because we been working all our life, the children, too. So I got in Welfare Rights.

Spanish-Speaking People and Welfare

I got on welfare when my husband left, and he left because there was three children in the family and he couldn't find a job to support them. This is the first of the Spanish-speaking people's problems—the father can get a job but it's not enough for the family. The rents would go high and the family has to pay for doctors and all these kinds of things, so he can't stay in one job. Also, he can't have a job that he would like to have, so he just takes off. He is so mixed up and at the same time he would like to have everything that the family needs.

The men get tired of little or no work and just go from city to city because they just can't take it and keep looking for a job to support the family. There are a lot of people who come to Milwaukee looking for work and when they can't find it they move on. Some take their families, but some leave them. At least the family gets some help from welfare. The people in Welfare Rights can explain to them their rights. A mother can get a full-time job and still get some help from welfare, but many don't know. If the Welfare Department would tell the people their rights, it would be different, but it's not that way.

In the Latin community, it is very hard to get on welfare, because the people don't know what is going to happen. They think their children will be taken away and their husbands will be put in jail with no reason. There are many Latins who could be on welfare but aren't because they don't know their rights. They're afraid. Now some are on welfare, but they think that they don't have have a right to this or that or even to see a man, or buy something. Like a mother spends the money on clothes for the kids and might not have it to pay the lights or gas, she is afraid she'll be cut off welfare.

I was afraid once, too, but not anymore. I was afraid that the caseworker would see my house and a few things would not be clean and she would drop me. In the first place she didn't understand me at all, because now I talk more English but I couldn't then and I was so shy because I had never talked to white people, because I had been working in the fields. When I first came on welfare, they didn't have any Spanish-speaking case-workers at all. Sometimes, I would just move my hands; now I know more English because I have had more time in Milwaukee.

When I came on welfare, caseworkers came every week to my house and checked everything and asked everything. They went through my whole house and checked to see no man was around. When I joined Welfare Rights, that stopped—because I learned my rights. When you learn your rights, you feel more free; you're not afraid.

There still are not enough Spanish-speaking casework-ers at the Welfare Department. Some whites can speak it, but they just know the language, they don't know the problems. Latins can understand better because they know, they have already passed through the same prob-lems. They know our culture.

Both men and women need good jobs. If you want to work, you should have a good job, not $1.60 an hour for a family, say, with five children. That is not enough to support the family. There are a lot of men and women out of jobs. They want jobs. The women in the house wants to do something because she sees that the husband doesn't get enough. But where can she get a job? She doesn't know the English, but she knows she can do something because she has worked in the fields.

Besides, the mother has got a job all the time, taking care of her children. It's a big job. She has to wash and cook and do everything because she has got to manage the house. If a woman can, she wants to have an outside job to help her husband, but she already has a job with the house and the children.

Better education, better jobs. I don't know why the Latins and other kinds of races got the worst problems. Because they're not educated, they don't know the language, and they don't know how to go around. Their jobs and everything were taken from them by machines.

Our children are dropping out, they don't know where to go. People come to the city looking for a better life. If they find better jobs, better houses, better living, they stay. If they see there is no chance, they just take off, they just go look around. Children are the same way, they drop out of school because they don't think they're ever going to get a job anyway.

If they can't get a job, they still have a right to live. But someone will have to be at the Welfare Department with them to tell them what their rights are. And you got to keep telling them because they never heard that before. They have never been taught their rights.

First, the man has to get a job because of the family —a decent job. If he can't, he has to be told his rights, to be proud and not worry. But he'll still be worried and afraid and will say, "Oh well, I had better go because the welfare's going to investigate me," because he never been investigated before.

With the children, either they know the English and don't know the Spanish or they know the Spanish and don't know the English. And they don't know where to go. Say a boy is qualified for a job when he finishes school. He knows both languages, but he's still not going to get a job because he's a Latin. In our community, lots of people finish school and still they don't get jobs. They go and apply for jobs and aren't called. They go again and again.

Caseworkers play games on us. I once asked for a bed

and the caseworker said it was coming but I never got it. Other mothers ask for washing machines (under the law, recipients can get them) and they never get them. Somebody has to go with them to talk, but still they don't get the things they need. There's a lady who asked for a washer a year ago and didn't get it. She doesn't know any English. All the time, she got to take her son or daughter out of school to go see the caseworker to talk English for her.

Then the child is missing school. She is going to get in trouble, but the caseworkers don't see that. Or if one of the children is very sick, the mother has got to take another one to talk to the doctor. After that, the child is getting flunked. Flunked, flunked, flunked, out. The school is going to put the blame on the mother. The counselors don't care if the children miss school. They don't give a damn.

Sometimes, when the child is missing school, they still pass him. We know the child is not learning. They pass the kids just to get rid of them, especially if they're on welfare. Because soon the welfare won't support them no more. If the child is in high school and he's going to be eighteen, he's going to be passed no matter if he's absent. It is not fair for the child. When he's eighteen, he no longer gets welfare. So they don't pay attention. My child is flunking, so he's quitting. This is not only my son, it's all the kids. They're good kids—not just because we're the mothers—they're really good kids. But they can't get a decent job because they don't have the education.

The schools are not teaching. They're too prejudiced. My daughter is nine years old. Her teacher gives her a hard time because I'm in Welfare Rights. Children are absent from school because they don't have any clothing, coats, boots, shoes, anything. I'm not going to send my kids to school if they're going to get sick on the way there, and this keeps them behind. Especially for the last two years when welfare won't give clothing, all my children are home in the winter—it gets down to 15 below in Milwaukee. They don't have anything to wear. This means the child goes down. If the child is on welfare, the school keeps him down, because he didn't have the money to pay for the books. In spite of all this, some kids try to go to school every day and still the teacher doesn't teach them. The child has to be very smart to get just a little thing.

But the child has to be educated before he can get anything. He's gonna go to school, and if he goes every day to school and doesn't get anything, he knows he's not getting educated. He'll drop out. Who's going to get blamed? The youth. The teachers still get their money for doing nothing. Our children are not getting educated at all in the schools. They finish school and they still don't know how to read or write.

That is why we are angry, that is why we fight. You need a good education to get a good job. People need a good job for a good living. But nobody is getting that. When a child can't get a good education no matter how he tries and because of that he can't get a job, and even if he has the education he still can't get a job, he has to have some support. This is the richest country in the world and people here have a right to live decent. So we have to have a guaranteed adequate income now.

8. Welfare Mythology

"A guaranteed adequate income? You must be
kidding. If you think we have troubles with our
present welfare system, a guaranteed adequate income system would multiply them a hundredfold.
You give those lazy, shiftless good-for-nothings
an inch and they'll take a mile. You have to make
it tougher on them. They're getting away with
murder now. You have to catch all those cheaters
and put them to work or put them in jail. Get
them off the welfare rolls. I'm tired of those niggers coming to our state to get on welfare. I'm
tired of paying their bills just so they can sit
around home having babies, watching their color
televisions, and driving Cadillacs."

No matter how much evidence is collected, no matter
how many studies are made, no matter how many government investigations are conducted disproving these ac-
cusations, people still believe them.

Why? Myths are needed to justify the welfare system,
a system that cheats the very people it is supposed to
help. Myths are needed to discourage eligible, low-paid
workers from applying for aid. Myths are needed to di-
vert taxpayer frustrations away from the country's big
welfare recipients—the rich and the military—and onto
the defenseless, powerless poor. In short, myths are needed
to hide the real welfare crisis.

Welfare myths are everywhere: on television and radio,

in papers and magazines, in songs. Even charitable institutions perpetuate the myths, precisely because they offer charity, rather than justice.

Six basic myths are used to hide the reality of welfare. All of them are contradicted by the facts. Yet they are used to capture the minds of the overburdened taxpayer, the low-income laborer, and even their target, the welfare recipient.

Myth: Hard Work Is the Answer to the Welfare Problem

This myth appeals most to the low-income laborer who is not getting paid enough to live decently. Rather than blame his employer for his plight, he is persuaded to blame the welfare recipient who does not work. However, the hard-work myth assumes that everyone on welfare is able to work. According to the U.S. Department of Health, Education, and Welfare, this is the composition of the national welfare caseload: [1]

24 per cent are old-age recipients (OAA);

8 per cent are permanently and totally disabled (APTD);

1 per cent are blind (AB);

50.3 per cent are children (AFDC);

2.9 per cent are incapacitated parents in homes (AFDC);

13 per cent are mothers (AFDC), of whom one-fifth are in job training or are employed already but are making so little money that they still qualify for aid; and

.8 per cent are able-bodied men, and these men have to be seeking jobs through their state employment agencies to get any aid at all.

The 24 per cent on old-age assistance are people who worked hard all their lives but never earned enough to pay the kind of social security premiums that would have provided them with adequate benefits when they retired or who worked in industries that did not provide social security or pension benefits at all. It is probable that some of these aged people could work and would like to work, but it is virtually impossible for them to find jobs at their age; employers won't hire them.

The next two categories—the 8 per cent permanently and totally disabled and the 1 per cent blind—comprise people who are, for all practical purposes, wholly unemployable.

As for the 50.3 per cent children, most of them are under eighteen, in school, and not considered eligible for the labor market. A few people still feel that, as soon as a child is old enough to earn an income, he should be put to work—that is, poor children should be put to work. More affluent families would presumably retain the right to keep their children at home. However, the majority of people still believe that education equals opportunity. Therefore, welfare children are not considered employable. Besides, there are no jobs for all these kids.

The next two groups—totaling 15.9 per cent—are the parents of these children. They are the real object of the first myth. It is said that, were these parents working, most of their children would also not be on welfare. One-fifth of these parents (2.9 per cent of all welfare recipients) are incapacitated. The remaining 13 per cent are the people who, it is insisted, must be put to work.

Well, they are being put to work. The present Federal AFDC Law demands "prompt referral to the Secretary of Labor or his representative for participation under a work incentive program . . . of . . . each appropriate child and relative who has attained age sixteen and is receiving aid to families with dependent children [42 USC 602 (a) (19) (A) (i)]." The Law further says that, if these appropriate children or relatives refuse to take part in the Work Incentive (WIN) Program or reject an offer of employment in which they are able to engage without a good reason, they shall be cut from the welfare grant.

The reality is that very few adult AFDC recipients can work, as a May 31, 1970, Monthly Status Report for WIN indicates:

Total Adult AFDC Recipients	Total Recipients Assessed	Appropriate for Referral by State Welfare Agency	Actually Referred by State Welfare Agency	WIN Enrollees After Labor Department Re-evaluation
2,150,000	1,810,578 (84.2% of total)	374,177 (17.4% of total) (20.7% of assessed)	282,380 (13.1% of total) (15.6% of assessed)	164,348 (7.6% of total) (9.1% of assessed)

As of that date, only 7.6 per cent of all adult AFDC recipients have been found to be appropriate for WIN training.[2]

But even those who might be appropriate for the training are not necessarily appropriate for work. In New York State, for example, only 17 per cent of WIN enrollees were placed in jobs and only 4 per cent remained employed beyond six months.[3]

"In Milwaukee County, the Welfare Department trained fifty AFDC mothers to be case aids, and when time came for the job 700 people applied so only two out of the fifty people that were trained were hired. I think it's up to seventeen now. But they had spent a quarter of a million dollars to train fifty mothers, and all the mothers got was training—no job."
Mrs. Hattie Shaw
Milwaukee, Wisconsin

Work training programs cost $6,000 per trainee.[4] Is it any wonder, then, that state and local governments would rather use the money intended for such programs for their own purposes? For another example, New York City's Offtrack Betting Corporation was financed by a $2.8 million loan from the Welfare Department's manpower training account, "with the proviso that the detailed plan for hiring minority contractors submitted by the New York Offtrack Betting Corporation be approved by the Manpower Career and Development Agency."[5] The loan was approved on January 4, 1971. Yet by the time $800,000 actually changed hands, it seems there was no such approved plan. This use of work-training funds bespeaks the perceived, and real, value of work-training programs.

"You can bet we see ourselves as some kind of political football, and we're tired of all the 'sportsmen' kicking us around."

Mrs. Garnette Reddic
Milwaukee, Wisconsin

But suppose that those who base welfare policy on the work myth have their way. In order for welfare mothers to have jobs, someone must take care of their children, so day-care centers will have to be provided. Then everyone should be satisfied—until the bill for the cost of running the day-care centers hits the taxpayer.

As of 1967, one out of every three children receiving AFDC was under six years old. A day-care program to cover all these children would cost this country $2.7 billion. If their mothers worked and were lucky enough to get the full minimum wage, their total earnings would be only $1.6 billion.[6] That leaves $1.1 billion as the net cost of day-care centers to society. Who would get that money? Not the _____ who need it, but the people who run t

Indeed, day-ca _____ graphically illus

If mothers o' the main job o Then, the mai taking care o own children former servic

Furtherm assumes th raising a f worthy of ing meals sick, budg children—all this is _____ knows.

Why, then, do welfare mothers get paid less _____ their job than anyone else? If a child is brought up in a public institution in Wisconsin, his guardian gets $9,600 a year. If that child is brought up—during the day—in a day-care center, the caretaker gets $1,915 a year.[7] A foster parent gets $1,500 a year to care for a child. But if the child's own mother brings him up in his own home, she gets only $660 a year. The government will pay the people in an institution or a foster home adequately to take care of a child, but it won't recognize the people who do the same job for the least amount of pay.

This country's economy is a service economy—public-service lawyers, doctors, dentists, social workers, teachers,

psychiatrists, and now day-care centerists. Wherever one turns, he sees new service companies springing up.

"If the government was smart, it would start calling AFDC 'Day and Night Care,' create a new agency, pay us a decent wage for the service work we are now doing, and say that the welfare crisis has been solved because welfare mothers have been put to work."

> *Mrs. Bessie Moore*
> *Milwaukee, Wisconsin*

Aside from their work in bringing up children, though, welfare mothers can't get jobs outside of the home; 82 per cent of all AFDC mothers have not completed high school, and 34 per cent have not gotten beyond eighth grade.[8]

But even if these mothers, somehow, were to get an education, they still would not be able to get jobs that would pay enough to get them off welfare.[9] In fact, they would be grossly underpaid for doing the same things men do, as Table 8.1 shows.[10]

Table 8.1 Income for Year-Round, Full-Time Workers, 1968

Occupation	Women	Men
Clerical workers	$4,002	$7,034
Operatives	3,506	6,209
Nonfarm laborers	2,984	4,165
Sales	2,248	7,396
Service	2,226	4,820
Private household	806	—

Most single mothers working in any of these jobs are eligible for welfare. The question, therefore, should not be who are on welfare when they should be working, but how many are working who should also be on welfare?

More importantly, welfare mothers cannot even get inadequately paying jobs. One-fifth of all welfare mothers are in the labor market, but 33.5 per cent of that group are unemployed—that is, they are looking for work but cannot find it; 33.5 per cent—over five times the national unemployment rate.[11]

In California recently, Governor Reagan wrote a letter to his state's 309,485 employers, asking each one to hire one welfare recipient. Of the 309,485, only 13,000 employers responded. And, of the 13,000, only 26 produced actual jobs—with an average weekly salary of $71, not enough to get any working mother off the rolls.[12]

Or take New York City, where a "get-tough" policy found 30,000 "employable" welfare recipients and forced them to pick up their checks at State Employment Centers and to take available jobs or be removed from the rolls. Even though the city later admitted that not all of the 30,000 *were* "employable," assume they were. That is only 30,000 people out of the city's 1.2 million welfare recipients that a "get-tough" policy can find as "employable." [13] That is 2.5 per cent of all New York City people on aid.

Again, the hard-work myth assumes that most people on welfare can work. The myth is true for .8 per cent of the national welfare caseload: the able-bodied men. However, as required by law, these men are already seeking employment.

The myth that hard work is the answer to the welfare problem is a tool used to control the minds of the worst-paid workers. They are made to see "being a bum on welfare" as the only alternative to their particular job. This belief becomes ludicrous when one realizes that these workers are themselves eligible for welfare, and not getting it. Such is the case in New York City, where 500,000 people—including cab drivers, the biggest complainers—are eligible, but not getting aid.[14] Such is the case for millions throughout the country.

Myth: Most Welfare Recipients Are Blacks Who Have Moved to Northern Cities Just to Get on Welfare

---

"Too many people are saying welfare's a black problem, when it's really a green problem. Why don't we have decent food, clothing, or shelter? It's simple. We don't have enough money."

Mrs. Rosie Hudson
Milwaukee, Wisconsin

Actually, the majority of welfare recipients are white— about 55 per cent, according to HEW. Thirty-nine per cent are black, and 6 per cent are American Indians and other minorities.[15]

During the two decades following World War II, some 20 million Americans moved from rural to urban areas. About one-third of these migrants were nonwhite, and most of them—about 90 per cent—did settle in the great northern cities. But they arrived expecting to get jobs, not welfare. During the peak migration period, 1950 to 1960, when large numbers of black people were moving north, the nation's welfare rolls rose only 17 per cent, despite the fact that male, nonwhite unemployment rates during the decade after the Korean War were particularly severe (9 to 13 per cent).[16] Large increases in the welfare rolls didn't begin until long after the peak period of migration had passed. The people who came on aid after 1965 were those who had been eligible for quite a while but were not yet on the rolls because they had been systematically denied their right to welfare.

Black people had moved north for a variety of reasons: in hope of better jobs, better education, less oppressive discrimination, and because they had nowhere else to go.

"Before I be a slave, I'm gonna walk away."
        Mrs. Christine Lee
        Milwaukee, Wisconsin
        formerly of Kosciusko, Mississippi

Or they moved simply to be near friends and relatives who had already gone north. Neither black people nor rural people in general have migrated to the northern cities just to get on welfare.

Myth: All Welfare Mothers Do Is Have Illegitimate Children

This is the most vicious of the welfare myths, because it generates the belief that welfare recipients are the "undeserving poor."

First, all welfare recipients do not have the proverbial

twelve children. The average welfare family has only 2.7 children, about the same as the national norm—2.4.[17]

The myth that welfare families have a lot more children than other families is used as a rationale against higher welfare benefits; as the argument goes, higher benefits would merely make having children more profitable.

"If you think that I'm gonna have a baby—and watch that child grow up with no food or clothing; and then watch him go to school where teachers don't teach him anything; and worry that he's gonna become a pimp or start shooting up dope; and finally, when he's raised, see him go into the army and get really shot up in there—if you think I'm gonna go through all that pain and suffering for an extra $50, or $100, or even $500 a month, why you must be crazy."

Mrs. Anne Henderson
Milwaukee, Wisconsin

Here a historical parallel may be illuminating. On May 6, 1795, at the Pelikan Inn in Speenhamland, Berkshire County, England, county magistrates formalized the first known guaranteed income program. Called the Speenhamland System, it attempted to provide workers with a supplement for low wages. In December of that year, the British Parliament passed legislation that enabled all counties to adopt a similar program.

The Speenhamland System was run on a county level and had two payment variables, the cost of bread and the size of the family. If, for example, a week's supply of bread cost one shilling, a worker or unemployed man was

83

to receive a weekly income of three shillings, plus one shilling, six pence for his wife and each additional family member.[18] The program paid the difference between wages and this minimum level out of the "poor rate."

In 1834, a Poor Law Study Commission made a severely critical Report on the Speenhamland System. One of its major criticisms was that it led to an increase in family size, since additional children brought higher benefits.[19] This criticism was completely false. The preamble to the 1821 British census had admitted that the system was "much less conducive to an Increase of Population than . . . usually stated to be in Argument." [20] Even Thomas Malthus, whose population theories caused much of the Commission's concern with birth rates, conceded, in the appendix to his 1826 edition of *Essay on the Principles of Population,* that the Speenhamland System did not in fact greatly encourage population growth.[21]

Besides making a false accusation, the commissioners of the Poor Law Report never even analyzed the questionnaires they used. Instead, the nine folio volumes of questionnaire results were attached to the back of the Report for opponents to review.[22] Such a review has shown that the commissioners conspired to produce a false report.[23]

America's welfare policies, based as they are on myths that are disproved by the government's own research, are no less of a conspiracy against today's poor. Nothing *has* changed.

But to return to the illegitimate-children myth: only 30 per cent of AFDC children are classified as illegitimate. This classification is possible only among those who refuse or are not able to conceal their sexual behavior by sudden marriages or abortions. Moreover, a recent report for HEW has shown that one-third of *all* first-born American children born between 1964 and 1966 were conceived out

Welfare Mythology

of wedlock; by the time these children were born, nearly 66 per cent of their mothers had married, making their children "legitimate." [24] Furthermore, an estimated 1 million abortions were performed in this country in 1969 alone.[25]

The fathers of illegitimate poor children cannot afford to marry, because they have no way to support their family; the "timely" marriage is a luxury denied the "undeserving poor." Welfare mothers realize full well the burden on their men, who are considered failures because they are not able to provide for their families.

"We have been forced, due to our sick society, to live as we are now. Fathers have been driven from their homes because of our welfare system which won't aid a family if the father is in the home. And then the government says the poor family is breaking up, and it's the one who's causing it."

Mrs. Roxanne Jones
Philadelphia, Pennsylvania

It is not welfare children who are illegitimate as much as it is an illegitimate society into which they have had the misfortune to be born, a society that refuses to provide decent jobs or income for men, but that condones and supports the prostitution of women.

Indeed, prostitution is legal in Nevada. And when that state made its illegal welfare cuts in January, 1971, social workers told welfare recipients to go to the whore houses and "work" there. Any Nevada welfare mother knows that this country's poverty program not only treats her like an urban prostitute, but it also tries to make her one.

85

"We're mothers, not whores."

Mrs. Johanna Bustamonte
Washoe County, Nevada

In sum, the illegitimate-child myth is this society's greatest projection of its own guilt.

Myth: Welfare Is the Good Life, Color TV's and Cadillacs

This myth is a projection of society's fantasies.

"You take the city of Omaha. That is home. Our part of the city looks like London during the blitz. And our youth didn't burn it down, either. The major firms have left, and an Armour cannery was partly demolished, and the rest was left standing—the boarded-up, rat-infested buildings were left standing for our children to view daily. They come home from school and wonder how we live in such a place."

Mrs. Lafern Williamson
Omaha, Nebraska

No one knows that this myth is a lie more than President Nixon, whose first cousins, Mr. and Mrs. Milhous, are on welfare in California. Mr. Milhous used to run a chain-saw business but was forced to stop because he had a heart attack in 1966. Now the family receives $270.10 a month in social security plus $51 a month in welfare payments. Yet even they had to get the services of a lawyer to force the state of California to provide them with a helper in the house, a service to which they were legally entitled.[26]

President Nixon's first cousins are far from a hardship case, especially when compared to other welfare recipients. Table 8.2 shows the December, 1970, average *monthly* grants for a welfare recipient under the five basic welfare programs.[27]

Table 8.2 Average Monthly Welfare Payments, December, 1970

Old-Age Assistance	Aid to the Blind	Aid to Families with Dependent Children	Aid to the Permanently and Totally Disabled	General Assistance
$77.60	$104.35	$49.50 per person $198 for a family of four	$96.55	$57.75

People who get these amounts are well off next to President Nixon's second cousin, Kathy Timberlake, who reports that she is getting only $27 a month from county aid in Cotati, California. She has written the President asking him if there is any way he can help her get more money.[28] She knows how much it costs to live in this country.

So do most Americans. A Gallup Poll released in January of 1971 revealed that people feel it costs at least $126 a *week* ($6,500 a year) for a family of four to make ends meet.[29] The U.S. Government's Bureau of Labor Statistics has agreed that this figure represents what is needed to live adequately at a *low* level in this country.[30] These cost estimates show that welfare is far from being the good life.

Except, of course, if the welfare recipient cheats.

Myth: Most Welfare Recipients Are Cheaters

Why shouldn't they be? This is a nation of cheaters. Cheating a little on your income tax is one form of casual, almost institutionalized fraud. There are many others, equally casual, equally acceptable, from padding expense accounts to short-changing highway toll machines. Almost everyone cheats, but rather than admit it, they look for scapegoats—welfare recipients.

And people judge others in terms of themselves; hence the rationale behind the welfare-recipients-are-cheaters myth. Table 8.3 shows one common kind of cheating—income-tax evasion.[31]

Table 8.3 Income Unreported, by Group, 1959

Group	Income Unreported	Per Cent of Income Unreported
Farmers, small businessmen, professionals (doctors, lawyers, etc.)	$12.0 billion	28
Wage and salary earners	6.5 billion	3
Receivers of interest	2.8 billion	34
Receivers of pensions and annuities	.6 billion	29
Receivers of rents, royalties, and capital gains	1.2 billion	11
Receivers of dividends	.9 billion	8

During a Welfare Rights demonstration for winter clothing in Milwaukee, a woman came up to condemn the action. "Welfare recipients have no right to complain," she said. She was a widow with four children, but, since her social security was not enough to live on, she had gotten a job as a waitress.

Mrs. Frankie Patterson told her, "If people can get a just wage and still raise their children decently, they should work. The problem is that no mother can get a just wage. How much do you make on your job?"

"I earn $1.10 an hour," the woman replied.

"Do you think that's a just wage?"

"No!"

"Well, if you want to submit yourself to an injustice, that's your privilege, but you shouldn't condemn us because we refuse to."

"Yes," she said, "but I get enough in tips to make up the difference. And besides, you all cheat."

"Do you pay taxes?" Mrs. Patterson asked.

"Yes, except on the social security. I don't have to pay taxes on that," she replied.

"But do you pay taxes on the tips you get?"

"Of course not! If I did that, I wouldn't be able to survive."

"Well then, you're cheating, because the law says you have to pay taxes on those tips. You're forced to cheat and that's an injustice. No one should be forced to cheat in order to survive. So why don't you join the rest of us cheaters and fight for a country where no one has to cheat in order to live?"

Despite the fact that they are the group of people with the most legitimate reason—survival—to cheat, welfare recipients do it less than anyone else. In fiscal 1970, only 0.7 per cent—7 out of every 1,000 welfare cases—were fraudulent.[32]

To be more specific, in New York City, where welfare eligibility statements are starting to be accepted without individual investigation, less than 2 per cent of applicants have misrepresented their cases.[33] Quite to the contrary, spot checks have revealed that erroneous rejections or illegal case closings have been more numerous than acceptances based on false claims.[34] And in Milwaukee, out of the 70,000 people receiving welfare in 1970, only 95 were found to be committing fraud.[35]

Just where are the welfare chiselers that the gentlemen in the cartoon are talking about?

And the bleeding that welfare has caused Uncle Sam is just a scratch. Despite the myth,

Myth: Welfare Takes Most of Your Taxes

Welfare, for the poor, does not.

For the fiscal year ending June, 1970, the total cost of welfare, including medical assistance, was $14.3 billion, of which $7.5 billion was federal money—less than 4 per cent of the federal budget.[36]

Compare welfare costs to warfare costs: for fiscal 1971, $73.6 billion, or 36.7 per cent of the federal budget, is scheduled for military programs.[37] The federal government spends five times as much on death and destruction as it does on life.

State and local governments provided the other $6.8 billion of the fiscal 1970 welfare payments. It is hard to generalize about the relative cost burden at these levels, but it is here that most complaints about taxes for welfare are centered. Yet certain things are clear. While no state in the union provides truly adequate welfare payments ("adequate" meaning $541 a month for a family of four), some states are vastly more inadequate than others; $70 a month for a family of four in Mississippi; $347 a month for such a family in New Jersey. But, in Mississippi, 78.6 per cent of fiscal 1970's public assistance expenditures

"*The miracle to me is that after being bled by these welfare chisellers so long Uncle Sam has anything left to bail out Lockheed <u>with</u>.*"

was paid with federal funds, whereas, in New Jersey, federal monies covered only 42.1 per cent of welfare costs.[38] In fact, the states that pay the lowest welfare benefits receive the highest percentage of their costs from the federal government.

Furthermore, the cities suffer most from the cost of welfare. For example, public assistance payments cost each Wisconsin resident $51.45 in fiscal 1970 (the national average cost per inhabitant is $61.90), but they cost each Milwaukee resident $99.[39] The lack of a uniform, adequate, federal welfare system, therefore, means that some Americans do have reason to complain about bearing an unfair share of the cost, as small as it is, of welfare.

Welfare myths are not only commonly believed by the average American but also are the foundation of the federal government's social and economic policies toward poverty. It is time these policies were based on reality. In reality, there is no reason for taxpayers to blame high taxes on the poor who get welfare. In reality, low-income laborers should demand *their* right to welfare. In reality, there should be a guaranteed adequate income in this country.

9. The "Experts'" Word Games

Guaranteed adequate income is not a new idea. "Experts" have been studying it for the past ten years. It would end poverty by providing benefits to those people working outside the home and not getting paid enough to live decently, to those working in the home and not getting paid at all, and to those unable to work. The following ways to provide such an income have been suggested: negative income tax, guaranteed minimum income, family allowance, and guaranteed adequate income. The first two will be discussed in this chapter.

Negative Income Tax Proposals

The negative income tax proposal has evolved from an analysis of the welfare provisions in the American tax system; it tries to make such provisions universal. The tax system affects only those people whose incomes are above a certain level—for a man with a wife and two children, this would be $3,000 or more a year (pre-1969 tax rates).[1] All families of four earning $3,000 or less a year pay no income taxes. Thus the present tax system does not include close to 25 million people in this country. Theoretically, a negative income tax would round out the tax system by introducing subsidies (negative taxes) at the lowest income levels as the counterpart to tax payments (positive taxes) at higher ones.

The negative income tax proposal also reflects the present income tax system's recognition of the need for a minimum income. Tax deductions and exemptions are just one way of saying that a family of four (pre-1969) requires $3,000 exempt from tax in order to exist at minimum subsistence; that a married couple in their middle years needs $1,600 to survive; and that an elderly, retired couple needs $3,000.[2] People who are unable to work, or who work but don't make these minimum amounts of money still have the same requirements for subsistence. Therefore, some sort of government subsidy is needed.

A negative income tax would be a cash payment to families or individuals whose incomes are below a specified minimum level, the amount determined by the size of the family's or individual's income, the established minimum income level, and the negative tax rate. There have been a number of negative income tax plans advanced by the "experts."

"They always find some people who have expertise about poverty but who aren't poor. Well, I ask you, if you're not poor, how can you really know anything about poverty?"
Mrs. Lola Sanford
Milwaukee, Wisconsin

The most basic plan was presented in 1962 by Milton Friedman of the University of Chicago, and it established the rationale (given above) for other such plans. It calls for a subsidy from the Department of the Treasury to each tax-reporting unit at the rate of 50 per cent of the amount by which the value of tax exemptions and deductions exceeds the pretax income of that unit—a guarantee of $1,500 a year for a family of four with no income. This means, for example, that a migrant farm worker with a wife and two children who earns $1,000 a year would receive a subsidy of 50 per cent of $3,000 minus his $1,000 earnings—in other words, $1,000. This subsidy would be added to his earnings to bring his total income to $2,000. For every additional dollar that the worker earned, the subsidy would be reduced by 50 cents—the 50 per cent negative income tax rate. This tax rate would apply until earnings reached $3,000 a year, the break-even income level. Table 9.1 shows the Friedman plan in operation.[3]

Table 9.1 Friedman Plan—for a Family of Four

Total Income Before Tax	Exemptions and Deductions	Taxable Income	Tax Rate (per cent)	Tax	Income After Tax
$ 0	$3,000	−$3,000	50	−$1,500	$1,500
1,000	3,000	−2,000	50	−1,000	2,000
2,000	3,000	−1,000	50	−500	2,500
3,000	3,000	0	50	0	3,000
4,000	3,000	1,000	50	140	3,860

Other versions of the negative income tax plan have been devised by Robert J. Lampman of the University of Wisconsin Institute for Research on Poverty. They differ according to the maximum subsidy payable and the negative income tax rate. One of them proposes a yearly allowance of $375 per person. For a family of four with no income, this is a guarantee of $1,500 a year. An income up to $1,000 a year would be taxed at 75 per cent; income between $1,000 and $2,000 would be taxed at 50 per cent; and income between $2,000 and $3,000 would be taxed at

25 per cent. Under this plan, the migrant worker earning $1,000 would receive the $1,500 plus $250 (the 75 per cent tax on his $1,000 would leave him with $250)—$1,750, for himself and his family. Table 9.2 spells out the Lampman plan. It differs from Friedman's only in that Lampman has added a decreasing negative income tax rate.[4]

Table 9.2 Lampman Plan—for a Family of Four

Total Income Before Tax	Allowance	Taxable Income	Tax Rate (per cent)	Tax	Income After Tax
$ 0	$1,500	$ 0	75	$ 0	$1,500
1,000	1,500	1,000	75	750	1,750
1,500	1,500	1,500	50	1,000	2,000
2,000	1,500	2,000	50	1,250	2,250
2,500	1,500	2,500	25	1,375	2,625
3,000	1,500	3,000	25	1,500	3,000

A third negative income tax plan has been formulated by James Tobin of Yale University. It would add tax credits to the income tax system.[5] Each person in a tax unit would receive $400 as an allowance, a yearly guarantee of $1,600 for a family of four. Additional income would be taxed at a rate of 33⅓ per cent. This tax rate would not end when benefits are equaled by earned income, which occurs at $4,800 for a family of four, but only when the 33⅓ per cent. and the regular tax rates produce the same tax payment. Table 9.3 shows that this occurs at $6,103 a year for a family of four, assuming a 14 per cent tax rate and pre-1969 exemptions and deductions of $3,000. Income above this level would continue to be taxed at the regular rate. People using the tax credit would not be able to use the regular tax exemptions or deductions under this plan. Here the migrant worker and his family would receive their $1,000 income plus the tax credit of $1,600 reduced by the tax of 33⅓ per cent of the $1,000, which leaves $1,267, for a total of $2,267.

Table 9.3 Tobin Plan—for a Family of Four

Family Income Before Federal Tax Allowance	Present Tax (—)	Tax Schedule Income After Tax	Tax (—) or Allowance	Proposed Schedule or Income After Tax or Allowance
$ 0	$ 0	$ 0	$1,600	$1,600
1,000	0	1,000	1,267	2,267
2,000	0	2,000	933	2,933
3,000	0	3,000	600	3,600
4,000	−140	3,860	267	4,267
4,800	−252	4,548	0	4,800
5,500	−350	5,150	−233	5,267
6,000	−420	5,580	−400	5,600
6,103	−434	5,669	−434	5,669

The Ripon Society has advanced a fourth negative income tax plan.[6] It provides "standard income allowances" based on the number of people in a family. The plan allows $1,500 a year for each adult, $1,500 for the first child, $1,000 for the second, $600 for the third, and $400 for the fourth, with a limit of $6,000 per family. The difference between a family's income and its "standard income allowance" would be its "poverty deficit." A negative tax of 50 per cent would be made on this deficit. The migrant farm worker earning $1,000 a year would have an "allowance" of $5,500 and a "deficit" of $4,500. The negative tax on this deficit would give the worker's family $2,250, for a total yearly income of $3,250. Table 9.4 shows the Ripon Plan. It would provide a higher minimum income—$2,750 a year for a family of four with no earnings—than any of the other negative income tax schemes.

Table 9.4 Ripon Plan—for a Family of Four

Earned Income	Deficit from Standard	Negative Income Tax	Total Income
$ 0	$5,500	$2,750	$2,750
500	5,000	2,500	3,000
1,000	4,500	2,250	3,250
1,500	4,000	2,000	3,500
2,000	3,500	1,750	3,750
3,000	2,500	1,250	4,250
4,000	1,500	750	4,750
5,000	500	250	5,250
5,500	0	0	5,500

All the negative income tax plans, however, are based on the mistaken assumption that poor people can "work" their way out of poverty. But, because of inadequate prevailing wages, the lack of decent, dignified jobs, the necessity for many to perform nonpaying work, and the inability of others to work at all, the poor *cannot* escape poverty merely by "working."

The negative income tax plans not only fail to guarantee anything close to an adequate minimum income, but they also fall desperately short of the U.S. Government's own 1971 poverty line, $3,800 for an urban family of four. What good are plans that fail to recognize that almost all of the people now receiving public assistance cannot work and are doomed to poverty unless they receive an adequate income? What good are plans that do not help people who already work but do not earn an adequate wage?

"We're sick and tired of all these 'experts' coming in and studying us. You know, if they gave us as much money as

The "Experts'" Word Games

they give all those people, we could do some pretty good
studies of our own. But if they gave us all that money,
there'd be no more poor people to study."

Mrs. Elizabeth Martin
Milwaukee, Wisconsin

Furthermore, none of the negative income tax plans set the goal of an adequate income for *all* Americans, and this omission is the crucial difference between negative income tax and guaranteed income programs. This difference is one of degree rather than kind, since negative income tax rates would also be used to offset earnings under a guaranteed income program.

The President's Commission on Income Maintenance Programs, set up in 1968 to study poverty in America, has presented a minimum income plan that illustrates the link between negative income tax and guaranteed income. The Commission suggested a yearly guarantee of $750 to each adult and $450 to each child in families with no income.[7] Any income beyond that would be taxed at 50 per cent until the break-even level.

Table 9.5 The President's Commission's Plan—for a Family of Four

Earned Income	Tax Rate (per cent)	Income Supplement	Total Income
$ 0	0	$2,400	$2,400
500	50	2,150	2,650
1,000	50	1,900	2,900
1,500	50	1,650	3,150
2,000	50 ·	1,400	3,400
3,000	50	900	3,900
4,000	50	400	4,400
4,800	50	0	4,800

Table 9.5 shows that the break-even level for a family of four in the Commission plan is $4,800 a year. Income above that would be taxed at the regular tax rate. This plan is the same as Friedman's, except that it has a higher guarantee level. The migrant worker and his family would receive $2,400 a year minus 50 per cent of his $1,000 income, which is $1,900, plus his income—for a total of $2,900.

The Commission's plan, like the other negative income tax programs, is completely inadequate; $2,400 a year for a family of four with no income is still far below the poverty line. Furthermore, it is no more than what the average family on welfare now receives. Yet, unlike the others, the Commission did endorse the principle of a full guaranteed adequate income:

> This level [$2,400 for a family of four] was not chosen because we feel that it is an adequate income, but because it is a practical program that can be implemented in the near future. The level can be raised to an adequate level within a short period of time. . . . The Commission strongly recommends that the benefit levels be raised as rapidly as is practical and possible in the near future.[8]

What the Commission did was to act as its own censor. It made a rational analysis of poverty in America, and then based its recommendations, not on that analysis, but on anticipated political reactions to the rational solution. Should the solution to a problem be designed for the problem, or for the reaction to the solution to the problem? The solution to poverty, and to the real welfare crisis, is a guaranteed adequate income: an amount of money that, by itself, would provide an individual or family with the basics needed to live adequately in this society.

Guaranteed Minimum Income Proposals

The following two minimum income plans are steps toward a guaranteed adequate income. One, developed by Robert Theobald, is the basic economic security (BES) system.[9] Like the negative income tax ideas, it proceeds from the understanding that income tax exemptions and deductions imply the need of a minimum income level. BES would provide a yearly "due income" of $1,000 for each adult and $600 for each child. For a family of four with no income, this would total $3,200 a year. Any earnings would be charged dollar-for-dollar against the guarantee, a tax rate of 100 per cent. In the final adjustment between earned income and BES, however, a premium of 10 per cent of earned income would be added, making the effective tax rate 90 per cent of income. Thus the migrant worker's family would get $3,200 from BES plus $100 (10 per cent of the husband's $1,000 earnings). Table 9.6 outlines such a family's earnings. It is open-ended because Theobald would coordinate the BES system with a Committed Spending (CS) system.

Table 9.6 Theobald Plan—for a Family of Four

Earned Income	Tax Rate (per cent)	Allowance	10 Per Cent Premium	Total Income
$ 0	0	$3,200	$ 0	$3,200
1,000	100	2,200	100	3,300
2,000	100	1,200	200	3,400
3,000	100	200	300	3,500
3,200	100	0	320	3,520

A second guaranteed income plan was created in 1964 by Edward Schwartz.[10] Under his plan, individuals and families would declare their projected income for the coming year. If that income were expected to fall below the federally guaranteed level, the individual or family would claim a family security benefit (FSB), which would provide $750 a year for each person without any income, or $3,000 for an urban family of four. However, the tax rates in this plan are high: 60 per cent on the first $1,000 of income, 70 per cent on the second $1,000, 80 per cent on the third, and 90 per cent on the fourth. The break-even point for a family of four is $4,000 a year, but regular taxes would not begin until the family has made more than $4,500, as Table 9.7 demonstrates.

Table 9.7 Schwartz Plan—for a Family of Four

Earned Income	Tax Rate (per cent)	FSB/Taxes	Total Income
$ 0–999	60	$3,000–2,400	$3,000–3,399
1,000–1,999	70	2,399–1,700	3,400–3,699
2,000–2,999	80	1,699–900	3,700–3,899
3,000–3,999	90	899–0	3,900–3,999
4,000–4,499	0	0	4,000–4,499
4,500–and above	regular tax rates on income above		4,500

Both the Theobald and Schwartz plans might discourage people from working. Their tax rates are so high—90 per cent for Theobald and 60 to 90 per cent for Schwartz—that it just would not pay to work under them. Moreover, both of these may be guaranteed income plans, but, like the others, they are far from guaranteed *adequate* income plans.

———

"People've been making up plans for the poor for years but the only ones who ever benefit from all these plans have been the people making them up. These plans, they're nothing

The "Experts'" Word Games

*but a bunch of word games that don't do anything—they
haven't put any more bread on our tables."*

Mrs. Marla Anderson
Milwaukee, Wisconsin

There are, however, four guaranteed income programs
that are more than just plans. The New Jersey Graduated
Work Incentive Experiment for urban families and the
Negative Income Tax Experiment for rural families are
two such. Both of these, funded by the Office of Economic
Opportunity, are being conducted by the Institute for Research on Poverty, University of Wisconsin. Two other
guaranteed income experiments are being conducted by
the federal government, the first by the University of Indiana in the Model Cities program in Gary, Indiana, and
the second by Stanford University in Seattle, Washington.

The New Jersey experiment is the only one to have
arrived at some conclusions.[11] Started in 1968, this study
is focusing on 1,374 families in Trenton, Passaic, Pater-
son, and Jersey City, New Jersey, and Scranton, Pennsylvania. The objective of the experiment is to measure the
effect of negative tax rates and income guarantees upon
the work incentive of urban residents. Therefore, it deals
directly with the fear that minimum income payments
will reduce the work effort of able-bodied males. The experiment, which covers only male-headed families, guarantees benefits to all except a control group, which receives nothing. And there is no requirement that the men
whose families get benefits accept work training or a job.

The experiment has two variables. The first is the
amount of the income guarantee, which ranges from 50
to 75 to 100 to 125 per cent of the poverty line for a

family of four. In 1968, this line was $3,300, but it was raised in both 1969 and 1970 to reflect yearly increases in the cost of living. The second variable is the rate at which the guaranteed amount is reduced as the family's income rises. This negative tax rate ranges from 30 to 50 to 75 per cent of income.

The experimental families have been divided into eight different guarantee and tax rate groups and then compared to the control group. The smallest guarantee was $1,650 for a family of four (50 per cent of the 1968 poverty line), with a tax rate of 30 per cent on additional income. The largest guarantee was 125 per cent of the 1970 poverty line for a family of four, or $4,608. Earnings under this guarantee were taxed at 50 per cent.

The New Jersey Experiment has made three preliminary conclusions.[12]

> 1. There is no evidence that work effort declined among those receiving income support payments. On the contrary, there is an indication that the work effort of participants receiving payments increased relative to the work effort of those not receiving payments.

People who previously worked all day without any chance of earning an adequate wage are, with the benefits from the experiment, able to start living decently. It is this possibility of having a *decent* life that gives one more incentive to work. Common sense tells us that it is not the man *with* a decent income who will not want to work, but the man without one who won't. Indeed, the guarantee has created a base from which fathers have found better jobs for better wages. This, in turn, has enabled their wives and children to stay out of the labor market, and thus promoted family stability.

2. Low-income families receiving supplementary benefits tend to reduce borrowing, buy fewer items on credit, and purchase more of such consumer goods as furniture and appliances.

The very poor must borrow money and make credit purchases in order to survive. Such buying habits, which to others seem foolish, are, in reality, wise, because they are the only ones possible. A mother on welfare in Wisconsin, for example, cannot get money for a kitchen table or a bed if hers wear out, so she has to borrow or buy on credit in order to get them—and she has to get them. Like everyone else, she stretches her money the best way she can.

3. The New Jersey Experiment can be administered at an annual cost per family of between $72 and $96. Similar costs for the current welfare system run between $200 and $300 annually per family.

Costs are reduced because most recipients can learn to administer their own program by filling out the necessary income reports, just as taxpayers prepare income tax returns. It's a lot more sensible—and a lot more just—for states to save money by hiring fewer social workers than by illegally reducing the benefits of recipients.

People are poor, not because they have no incentive to work or don't spend their money wisely, but because they do not have enough money. It *is* that simple.

10. Zap FAP I

"We know that it is unpopular for welfare recipients, as they say, to bite the hand that feeds them. But the fact is that the President's three dogs get to live off $2,700 a year— three dogs—which is much more than $1,600 for a family of four. The point is if you don't have enough in that hand, you bite it off. If they had fed us, had something in that hand that we could taste as we bit, we wouldn't have no problem. But the point is you have a hand sticking out there, man, but there is nothing in the hand, so we are going to bite it off."

Mrs. Johnnie Tillmon

President Nixon has offered a family allowance program to the country—the Family Assistance Plan (FAP). As presented in 1970, FAP I (the first version) would have provided $500 a year for each of the first two members of a family and $300 a year for each additional member, or $1,600 a year (plus $864 worth of food stamps) for a family of four. Under FAP I, the first $720 of yearly income would not have been taxed. After that, earnings would have been taxed at a rate of 50 per cent until the tax canceled out the allowance. For a family of four, as Table 10.1 shows, this would have occurred when earnings equaled $3,920 a year.

Zap FAP I

Table 10.1 First Nixon Family Assistance Plan—for a Family of Four

Earned Income	Benefit	Total Income
$ 0	$1,600	$1,600
720	1,600	2,320
1,500	1,210	2,710
2,500	710	3,210
3,500	210	3,710
3,920	0	3,920

"Who is it that had the audacity to sit down over Scotch on the rocks or whatever you have, pills or Benzedrine or whatever it is, and even consider in this affluent and rich country, where we waste over $70 billion a year in military, that a family of four should live on $1,600? I want to get to him."

Mrs. Roxanne Jones

The *real* experts on poverty know how FAP I would have affected the poor.

Statement by Mrs. Beulah Sanders, New York City
National Chairman, National Welfare Rights Organization

The National Welfare Rights Organization opposes FAP unless its major defects are remedied.

Number one, the principle that every person has a right to an adequate income must be recognized. Adequate income must be defined at $6,500. This is the minimum needed by a family of four to live. The so-called poverty line is inadequate and we reject that because we feel that it is inadequate compared to our statistics. Under FAP, only families with children are eligible. There is a separate program at higher benefits for the aged, disabled, and blind. Everyone else, childless couples and single individuals, would not be covered—they will have to rely on almost nonexistent local relief. The *right* to an adequate income should extend to all people.

Number two, no benefits currently going to recipients can be curtailed or cut out. In some states, there are special needs (items which can be obtained when needed—stoves, refrigerators, etc.) and they will be cut out if the Family Assistance Plan is passed. FAP I would increase benefits for only 13 per cent of the welfare families, freeze benefits for 60 per cent, and possibly cut benefits for the 27 per cent that live in states paying more than the poverty level. Recipients in New York, Alaska, Connecticut, Massachusetts, New Jersey, and Pennsylvania could be cut.

Number three, provisions of the bill which encourage the disintegration of families must be eliminated. We feel mothers of school-age children must not be required to leave their children for jobs. We also feel that the stepfathers must not be made liable to support their stepchildren; otherwise, the woman stands a chance of losing out on a husband, which she could have had, through the man being forced to take care of those kids. We feel our mothers need husbands as well as any other citizen.

Number four, the Family Assistance Plan must not be a vehicle for subsidizing slave-wage employers at the expense of poor people. What we are talking about is the forced work law which is going to create a number of problems. I don't feel that welfare mothers should be forced out of their homes, because 90 per cent of them are in the home alone with their children. If the administration can come up with adequate jobs and adequate training, we will not have to be *forced* to go to work. This FAP is not doing that. What it is telling us is that we must take any kind of job in order to satisfy the Nixon Administration. I think the President needs to get him some credibility somewhere else, not off the backs of poor people.

Number five, the constitutional rights of poor people must be protected. Under FAP, they are not. Recipients would not even be entitled to a fair hearing. Come on, this country can do better than that.

And I found out something the other day that shocked me: 90 per cent of our representatives are millionaires or damn near millionaires. They're not poor, so therefore they know nothing about problems like poverty. They went to school and got those degrees and they all, 90 per cent of them, were lawyers. So they ran for office and they are sitting up with their cocktails making up laws which they say are going to be beneficial to us and they haven't even asked us. That is my concern. I don't think that this country can any longer set policy for law and order without asking people first . . . the people that they are setting those policies for.

When the Constitution was set up, it meant that people had to go to a poll and pull a lever to put the politicians in office and the only way we are going to have to deal with those politicians is to let them know, "We vote now, baby. It used to be that we didn't, but we do now."

Welfare Mothers Speak Out

"I was at a seminar in Philadelphia, and somebody in Washington sent an unlearned, uninformed cat there to sell the FAP bill. Don't send him no more. This man, I asked him, 'Who is it that thought up the $1,600 figure?' He couldn't tell me. Maybe it was because 1600 Pennsylvania Avenue is the address of the White House."

Mrs. Roxanne Jones

Statement by Mrs. Edith B. Sloan
National Committee on Household Employment

For those of you who do not know what a household worker is, she is your present-day house slave or house darkie, your Aunt Jemima. She is the lady who does your laundry, who cleans your house, who looks after your children, who does your cooking, who says, "Yes, ma'am," and calls you all "Miss Jane."

We know what it is to live on $1,600 a year. The median wage for household workers in this counrty is $1,523 a year, or less than $126 a month, or about $37 a week. Our average age is 46.

According to statistics, there are about 1.6 million of us, but we know better. There are really about 2 or 3 million. Most of us are black. We do not even know how many Chicanos or Indians there are. And all of us are very poor. We know that you cannot live on $1,600 a year.

We know that if the President's Family Assistance Plan goes through, many of the women who are welfare mothers will be forced into our labor force. It would be a catastrophe. In a few years that the National Committee has been in existence, we have managed in a few places, for example, down in Raleigh, North Carolina, to get the wages raised from $35 a week to maybe $60 or $65. Of course, most of the household workers are in the South, over half of them. And we feel that with this Family Assistance Plan, which would force 3 million more mothers to work, many of the welfare mothers will be forced into household employment. We feel that this will just cut the wages back to $35 a week.

And where we have not been able to reach the women yet, in the Delta and the Southwest, and around the reservations, and so forth, it will make it even worse. Not only will it wound them financially, it will kill them spiritually, because if there was even a little gap in that circle of poverty there from which they could escape, FAP I will close it.

Statement by Mrs. Josephine Heulitt
National Committee on Household Employment

For twenty years, I have seen the struggling mother caring for her little ones and dragging them out into the cold, trying to say she is not a welfare recipient, making less than $35 a week, living on less than that, and paying her transportation, clothing, and no Medicare whatsoever for her children, and no shoes—just to go out and do somebody else's work which has been called a dirty job. They have no social security, and they are not covered by any kind of law such as a minimum wage. They have no unemployment compensation. In case one works twenty years and her employer, say a Mrs. Smith, dies and she no longer is needed, where does she go? And you wonder why society in America has decided to put these people aside. We vote, we pay taxes. It is beyond my belief to understand how this many people have been lost.

Welfare Mothers Speak Out

I know the statistics on household employment are not right. Why? I, myself, have never registered through an employment officer. People all call up this Mrs. Smith and say, "Well, how about your girl"—that is how we are referred to—"does she know someone that we can get to work?"

Now social security, that is supposed to be a law. But if someone decides to pay me out of his pocket, and make me believe that he is giving me a few cents more, he does, and I am not able to cope with the law—remember, I am a household worker—and he is supposed to know what the law is about, but he is beating it.

And if anyone tells you that they don't know what a household worker is, don't believe them. Because most people in this country have had one that has raised them, is still raising their children. And if you don't believe that we have a hold in this country, let us stay home for a day and see what happens to your offices and homes.

"We want jobs, we need jobs. And we poor people want to work. But we do not want to give up our rights, our dignity and life, and then go and get the lowest wages for the job which will not adequately take care of, or benefit in the way of helping, our children."

Mrs. Marie Bracey
Wetumfska, Alabama

Statement by Mrs. Roberta Scott, Missouri

President Nixon's Family Assistance Plan is supposed to help the state of Missouri. In the state of Missouri, a family of four would get $133 a month from it. Now, I am from Missouri, that is the "show me" state, and I want someone to show me how FAP I is going to help my people in Missouri.

I am one of the working mothers on welfare. At the present time, my income from working and a welfare grant is $5,202. This is for a family of five. The government's own Bureau of Labor Statistics says a family of four needs at least $6,500 a year. And I am not making that now. If Nixon's plan were to go into effect today or tomorrow, my total income would then be $3,931 a year, a cut of $1,371. Now, show me how Nixon's plan is going to help me, when it is going to cut my grant and I am working. I am eligible, right now in Missouri, for a grant of $1,860 a year, but under Nixon's plan, I would be eligible for only $589. I am not the only working mother in the state of Missouri. There are many of us. And Nixon is going to sit there and say FAP is going to help us.

All the people who are supposed to be representing the poor, who sit in Washington, and sit in the state legislative positions, and say "We know what is good for the people"—well, they don't know what is good for the people. We know what is good for us. And it is time this stopped. It is time that all the politicians listened to the people.

11. Zap FAP II

The first version of the Family Assistance Plan was never voted on during the 1970 session of the Senate and so it died. Nixon, however, made certain changes in the bill and reintroduced it to the 1971 Congress as his top priority. FAP II would be even worse than FAP I, but by June, 1971, it had passed the House of Representatives.[1]

FAP II would, for the first time, provide aid to families with an unemployed father in the home, and it would raise the payment level for recipients in states that now pay the least. But it would not be a step toward welfare reform—it would be a brutal step backward.

Zap *FAP II*

FAP II proposes a "guaranteed income" of $2,400 a year for a family of four and allows recipients to keep the first $720 of yearly earnings plus one-third of their income beyond that. Table 11.1 shows that the most a family of four could receive in wages and/or welfare from this program is $4,320 a year.

Table 11.1 Second Nixon Family Assistance Plan—for a Family of Four

Earned Income	Assistance	Tax Rate (per cent)	Total Income
$ 0	$2,400	0	$2,400
720	2,400	0	3,120
1,020	2,200	66⅔	3,220
1,620	1,800	66⅔	3,420
2,220	1,400	66⅔	3,620
3,120	800	66⅔	3,920
4,320	0	66⅔	4,320

FAP II would not increase the amount of money that 90 per cent of America's welfare recipients have to live on. Its $2,400 does sound like more than the $1,600 a year in FAP I, but FAP I's $1,600 would have been supplemented by $864 in food stamps. FAP II cuts out the food stamps and does not require the states to maintain their value in benefits to recipients. In fact, FAP II would not even require states to maintain their present welfare payments; states would be free to cut back payments so that the $2,400 from the federal government would be all that a welfare family of four could receive.

FAP II would provide higher benefits for the welfare families who receive the lowest payments, but where are these families located? In Alabama, Arkansas, Florida, Georgia, Kentucky, Louisiana, Mississippi, South Carolina, Tennessee, Texas, and West Virginia. But right now the federal government pays nearly 75 per cent of all the welfare costs in these states, anyway. Under FAP II, the federal government would pay all costs. Yet, at the same time, the plan would hardly reduce the welfare costs in states such as New Jersey, Illinois, Michigan, Massachusetts, Connecticut, Pennsylvania, and New York—unless such states drastically cut their current grants.[2]

FAP II does not exist by itself, though. It would offer benefits only to those families whose employable members are enrolled in the Opportunities For Families program, trying to get OFF welfare. What does *employable* mean? For FAP II, it means that mothers with preschool-age children (children age three or over) will be forced out of the home and required to take any job.

Remember now, in order for such welfare mothers to "work," there would have to be a national day-care program, a day-care program that would not only free mothers to go to work but also hire the ones who have been freed.

But FAP II would require families using the child care services to pay for all or part of the costs involved. Since the program itself provides nowhere near enough money for such services, a mother would end up paying the day-care center to pay her to watch her own children—and other's, of course. Welfare would have created a new form of slavery: institutionalized, partially self-employed nannies. And these nannies would get only three-quarters of the minimum wage.

———————

"Can't you imagine it? A mother of two children, say, aged three and four, would get up in the morning, dress herself and her kids, walk or take a bus to the day-care center, watch, feed, and work with her children between 9 and 5,

dress them up again, go home, and take care of them the rest of the day. Between 9 and 5, she would be 'working in a day-care center,' and the rest of the time she would be just a 'mother.' How ridiculous."

                                            Mrs. Betty Glosson
                                            Milwaukee, Wisconsin

---

FAP II also tries to void the legal rights of the poor. Hearings to challenge Welfare Department decisions would be subject to final review by the secretary of HEW, not by the court. To give any bureaucracy, especially the welfare bureaucracy, that kind of power over a person's life is completely unconstitutional.[3] And FAP II gives the secretary broad authority to ban certain people—such as Welfare Rights advocates—from representing recipients in the hearing process. Finally, FAP II gives the secretary the power to appoint hearing examiners who do not even meet the Administrative Procedure Act's standards for such. This would turn the position into another plum of political patronage—at the expense of poor people's lives.

Applicants for welfare would be brutally mistreated under FAP II. Families who lost their jobs could be denied assistance for six to nine months because FAP II assumes they have savings—even if all their savings have been used up. FAP II would force eligible families to make separate applications for FAP and other benefits, such as Medicaid, state supplemental payments, if any, and surplus food commodities. Finally, FAP II encourages states providing more than $2,400 a year for a family of four to reimpose unconstitutional residency requirements.

And FAP II would unjustly harass welfare recipients. Benefits would be automatically stopped unless a family submitted an income report within thirty days after the end of a quarter-year during which it got aid, and the family would be fined for reporting late. Recipients would be automatically cut off welfare and forced to reapply for it every two years, though no one might challenge their continued eligibility. But FAP II does not even require that recipients be told of these changes in the law.

The Nixon Administration, however, is making one attempt to eliminate poverty; the Census Bureau is replacing "poverty" with "low-income level." [4] A 1971 Census Report has shown a dramatic increase in poverty in this country—politically embarrassing; yet the best way the administration can think of dealing with it is with a word game.

But again, it is the experts who really know about FAP II:

Statement by Mrs. Shirley Rivers, Maryland

As it has been for so many years, welfare people have been talked about, pushed around, shoved aside, and the husbands and men have been forced out of the homes. We just don't have anything.

This country has what we call the army, where they draft our friends, our sons, and our husbands. They have no say in the matter. The government tells us to be good mothers: raise your children. We raise our children, especially the boy children, and then they are taken from our homes and sent over to some foreign land to fight a battle that we don't know a thing about, ain't none of our people. This country spends $6,500 for three seconds of war and then talks about $2,400 for a family of four for a year. Now what kind of sense does that make?

But that is only one thing. I am telling you right now I also have a daughter in high school, sixteen years old, in the eleventh grade. She types ninety words a minute. Do you think for one second if I hadn't been able to inspire my child to the best of my ability, do you think she would be there?

And if you think for one minute that crime is on the increase, and that dope is flying around here, and that people get knocked in the head, now, honey, if FAP II passes, hang it up, just hang it up, because that stuff is going to be all over. Yeah, I can see somebody taking dope to forget about FAP.

People want to think that welfare recipients are the cause of all these slum areas; we are the cause of all this, everything that is bad—poor people, black people, poor white trash, and illiterate welfare people are the cause of it. It is the politicians that have been making these welfare decisions for so many years that are the real cause.

Statement by Mrs. Mildred Prem, Buffalo, New York

People in this society cannot sit up on a full stomach, with shoes, good clothes, beautiful homes, and paradise, and give us hell. It will not continue, because our children were born to destroy society if people do not change it. And do not let FAP II in or we will be destroyed along with it.

I want to tell you that the system itself is set up to perpetuate welfare. I want to tell you that business is what the government is backing, and keeping cheap labor pools and low salaries. Pre-emancipation is what we have. Slavery is slavery no matter what word you give it, or how you phrase it. And that is where we are at. And no one should send children to school and tell them that they can be educated, and then have them go hungry, and live in the riot areas—and riots mean the deterioration of society itself.

Welfare has created jobs, but not for the poor; it has created middle-class jobs—psychiatrists, sociologists, policemen, social workers, commissioners, and so forth, all the way to penal institutions.

And there are going to be more such jobs if FAP goes in, because there will be a hell of a lot of people going to jail. And there you go, all sorts of social workers, and more doctors and psychiatrists, all running in a circle.

And I want to say something about our rights in the evasive East, which keeps us all fooled, where the liberals are. It is no different in the East than it is in the West, than it is in the South, than it is in the North, because we have the same problems everywhere.

We stand in the rain to get food stamps in Buffalo—just the same as in Mississippi. We are sent over to a line, and there is confusion, and there is another food stamp window, and you do not know where to look, you think it should be over there to the right, but this time it might be to the left or in the basement. One day I expect to see it up in the Senate, because every time you go in *there*, there is confusion. You have got to ask where the food stamp window is. They put a little sign up there, and it takes a long time to find it. And they treat you like they are giving you a great gift. It's the rich farmers that are getting the great gift.

Down South it is so hard to get on welfare, it is almost like your sister and your mother have got to be working for the church or the governor or somebody. And I know that FAP II will enslave these people even more so.

It is hard to get on welfare in the South, it is hard to get on welfare in Buffalo. You just don't go down there and say, "We want to be on welfare." You may go down and it will take you three weeks. And in three weeks you can die.

We were wrong for allowing the politicians to have much power. The way to keep a beautiful country is for there to be even control, everybody have a section of it.

And the family is the backbone of every country. And next to the family comes business. Let us stop putting business first and family last, because if you have no strong family, you have no country. You just have a lot of puppets that the government is controlling, and then somebody else can come in and control them.

12. $6,500 or Fight

There is a welfare crisis in the United States today. Despite the growing number of poor people finding out about their right to welfare, 12 million people are still not on the rolls. Another 25 million people are struggling along without an adequate income. One-fourth of the country's population cannot afford the basic necessities of life: food, clothing, and shelter. Yet the country is unwilling to consider the one solution that will truly eliminate poverty—Guaranteed Adequate Income.

NWRO challenges the government to change its priorities from death and destruction to life and peace. We call upon the government to stop subsidizing the rich, the corporations, and the military, and start assuring an adequate income for all Americans—through wages, welfare, or both.

In 1969, when NWRO first devised its Guaranteed Adequate Income (GAI) Plan, a family of four needed $5,500 a year to survive at a minimum but adequate level of health and decency. Today, it takes $6,500. The change from $5,500 to $6,500 is not a change in the plan; it is simply that grant levels have been adjusted to reflect the rise in U.S. living costs.

Welfare Mothers Speak Out

"We are not an organization of selfish people and we are not out to get things done just for Welfare Rights or members of our organization. We, as an organization, want to see some guaranteed adequate income for all people in the United States of America."

Mrs. Beulah Sanders

$6,500 a year for a family of four—the GAI base grant —was computed on the basis of surveys conducted by the U.S. Department of Labor's Bureau of Labor Statistics (BLS). These surveys, as reported in Labor Department Bulletin No. 1570-5, "Three Standards of Living for an Urban Family of Four Persons," reflect the approximate amount of money that a family of four must spend for the "maintenance of health and social well-being, the nurture of children, and participation in community activities."

The report outlines three budgets at three different levels: low, moderate, and higher. NWRO's Guaranteed Adequate Income Plan is based on the lower living standard budget, which generally allows a family of four to have access to decent standards in housing, transportation, clothing, and personal care.

However, NWRO rejects the lower living standard's food budget, which is based on the U.S. Department of Agriculture's "low-cost food plan," since government surveys show that 70 per cent of the families with food budgets equivalent to the low-cost food plan have nutritionally inadequate diets. Therefore, the $6,500 budget uses the Agriculture Department's "moderate food plan," which would assure an adequate diet for every American. Providing an adequate income is the only way to combat hunger in America.

In calculating its budget, NWRO specifically rejects the official poverty level as a measure of what a family needs to live at a minimally adequate level. The poverty level was devised by the Social Security Administration on the basis of the Agriculture Department's economy food plan. But the Agriculture Department has said that the economy food plan "is not a reasonable measure of basic money needs for a good diet. The public assistance agency that recognizes the limitations of its clientele and is interested in their nutritional well-being will recommend a money allowance for food considerably higher than the cost level of the economy plan."

But the Social Security Administration merely took the cost level of the economy food plan and multiplied it by three to determine the total "poverty level" budget for a family of four. It not only ignored the Agriculture Department's warning, but it also disregarded the BLS's finding that a family of four needs a total budget closer to four or five times the cost of its food component. Table 12.1 shows how the $6,500 budget is broken down.

It should be noted that the budget excludes the basic cost of hospital and doctor's care, since it is assumed that free medical care will be available through Medicaid, national health insurance, or some other program. It should also be carefully noted that this is a minimum adequacy budget, providing only a basic subsistence income. There is no allowance for things like life insurance, out-of-town travel, a car, cigarettes, long-distance phone calls, or use of a laundromat.

The Guaranteed Adequate Income Plan would not be

Table 12.1 Minimum Adequate Budget for a Family of Four

Category	Year	Cost Per Month	Week
Food: This allowance is a total of the BLS moderate budget cost for food at home ($2351/yr., $196/mo., $45/wk.) and the BLS lower standard for food away from home ($279/yr., $23/mo., $5/wk.). The latter includes snacks, school lunches, etc.	$2,630	$219	$50
Housing: These costs represent the BLS lower standard's costs, updated to spring, 1969, levels. They are meant to cover all supplies and furnishings for a home and its operations, including telephone and postage. Rental costs ($1,303/yr., $108/mo.) include all items such as gas, electricity, and water.	1,648	137	32
Clothing and personal care: The items in this budget, such as shampoo and yard goods, as well as clothing and clothing care, are unchanged from the BLS lower standard. The cost has simply been updated for cost-of-living increase.	922	76	18
Medical care: Dental and eye care and nonprescription drugs are included here. BLS consideration of doctor and hospital care has been omitted, as explained in the text. There is no provision for medical appliances or supplies.	367	30	7
Transportation: Includes school bus rides and all other use of public transportation by non-car-owners.	569	47	11
Other: Reading, recreation, and education comprise about half of this category. There is no provision for life insurance, club membership dues, hobby expenses, or the acquisition of musical instruments.	379	32	7

limited to families, however. All Americans would be assured of a basic standard of income and payments would vary according to family size (see Table 12.2). And, to prevent families who are receiving Guaranteed Adequate Income Plan payments from becoming poorer as prices and the average family's income go up, the payment level would be adjusted annually to reflect both the rise in the cost-of-living and the increase in the median family income.

Table 12.2 GAI Plan's Payment Levels for Different-sized Families

Family Size	Year	Income Per Month	Week
One person	$2,250	$188	$ 43
Two people	4,100	342	79
Three people	5,300	442	102
Four people	6,500	542	125
Five people	7,700	642	148

$1,200 a year for each additional family member

In rural areas and in the smaller urban centers, the amounts would be less than shown above, while in large cities, the amounts would be higher. The $6,500 is an average urban budget. Table 12.3 shows figures for specific cities.

The Guaranteed Adequate Income Plan also provides emergency grants for clothing and furniture to bring participants' households up to minimum standards of health and decency at the time they first come into the plan. Replacement costs are provided in cases of flood, fire, or any other substantial change in the family's circumstances.

The Bureau of Labor Statistics assumed, in computing its budget, that the family had been established for fifteen years and had accumulated stocks of clothing and furni-

Table 12.3 GAI Plan's Payment Levels for Different Cities

Area	Amount Per Year
Urban United States	$6,500
Nonmetropolitan areas	6,110
Atlanta	5,980
Baltimore	6,565
Boston	6,890
Chicago	6,760
Cincinnati	6,175
Cleveland	6,630
Dallas	6,240
Denver	6,240
Detroit	6,500
Hartford	7,085
Honolulu	8,060
Houston	6,045
Indianapolis	6,630
Kansas City	6,500
Los Angeles	7,020
Milwaukee	6,630
Minneapolis	6,695
Nashville	5,915
New York	6,695
Philadelphia	6,500
Pittsburgh	6,240
Saint Louis	6,500
San Francisco	7,150
Seattle	7,150

ture, and thus its budget was intended only to cover replacements. This assumption does not apply to the average family in poverty, making emergency grants for furnishings and wardrobe necessary to bring persons up to minimum standards of health and decency and to meet disasters if they occur.

Most of the recipients of guaranteed adequate income would be working people who do not earn adequate wages. The GAI Plan provides a work incentive by allowing them to retain the entire cost of all expenses made in connection with the job, such as child care, transportation, uniform and tools, and union dues, plus one-third of their earnings above this amount. An amount equal to the remaining two-thirds would be deducted from the GAI payment.

For example, if a man with a wife and two children earns $100 a week above his work-related expenses, two-thirds of this amount would be deducted from the GAI payment of $125 a week for a family of four. They would be left with a payment of $125 less $67–$58. This would be $58 more than they would get without the Guaranteed Adequate Income Plan. No forced-work requirement is necessary. People will, and do, work if given a good opportunity.

Under the GAI Plan, a family of four would be eligible for benefits until its earned income reaches just under $12,000 a year. Families earning up to $9,750 would receive actual payments as described above. Families earning over $9,750 would also benefit because they would pay income taxes at a reduced rate until their earnings reach $11,461. At this point, a family of four would begin paying taxes at the normal rate. Table 12.4 compares the final income of a family of four under the GAI Plan with the present federal income tax law at various earning levels.

Participants in the Guaranteed Adequate Income Plan would also have the right to choose between the basic payment level of the plan or an itemized budget of their own needs, which would take into consideration the actual costs of housing, clothing, or any special problem not reflected in the basic budget. This is similar to the income tax system in which an individual can take the standard deduction or itemize his or her deductions, whichever gives greater benefits.

The GAI budget is based on statistical averaging formulas that do not necessarily apply to real people or real situations. For example, an individual family of four may or may not be able to obtain adequate housing in good condition at the $92 a month rent that the budget allows, even if that happens to be the average for the city in which they live.

Table 12.4 GAI Plan Compared to Income
Under Present Tax Law (Through 1971)
for Family of Four

Earnings	GAI Plan Payment	Final Income Under GAI Plan	Income Under 1971 Tax Law
$ 0	$6,500	$ 6,500	$ 0
2,000	5,167	7,167	2,000
3,000	4,500	7,500	3,000
4,000	3,833	7,833	4,000
5,000	3,167	8,167	4,860
7,500	1,498	8,998	6,476
9,000	500	9,500	7,589
9,750	0	9,750	8,231
10,000	−167	9,833	8,445
11,461	−1,114	10,317	10,317

Furthermore, GAI would provide clear protections against the kind of harassment that prevents the poor from receiving aid under the present welfare system. Eligibility would be based solely on need and would be determined by a person's simple declaration of his needs, with spot checks, as in our income tax system. All rights and regulations under the Guaranteed Adequate Income Plan would be written in simple and understandable language. The plan would be administered by a single agency, located in the federal government, with uniform standards and procedures throughout the country.

Participants in the plan would be entitled to a fair

hearing prior to the reduction or termination of benefits, the hearing to take place within fifteen days of the application for appeal. Special grants would be provided for legal fees, child care, and other expenses associated with appeals. Fair-hearing decisions could be appealed in the courts.

Services of all kinds, controlled by the participants, would be available, including family and vocational counseling, homemaker services, family planning, child care, other educational programs, and legal and medical services. While making no specific provisions for them, GAI assumes that these services would be free and located in the recipient's community, as they should be in a truly civilized society.

NWRO's Guaranteed Adequate Income Plan would provide benefits in the form of actual payments, work incentives, or tax relief to a little over half the people in this country—112 million, according to estimates made by the Department of Health, Education and Welfare.

Yearly costs of the program would be $72.4 billion. That is a lot of money. It is a lot more than Congress is currently willing to spend on poor people, but it is not much compared to the welfare Congress provides the military, the rich, and the big corporations. And GAI could be paid for simply by reducing the benefits that these groups get from the government.

But $6,500 a year for a family of four is not a lot of money; it is merely what is needed to live adequately at a low level in this country.

"If this country is going to reform welfare, for crying out loud, reform it so we can live and not die."

Mrs. Lee Williams

13. Guaranteed Adequate Income Now

by Mrs. Cassie B. Downer
Chairman, Milwaukee County Welfare Rights Organization

The family is the basis of the American society, but we are moving away from the family because people are forced out of the home in order to get an adequate income. My mother always did domestic work. She took care of someone else's children and we had to raise our own selves. My father always worked two jobs. One job he worked six days a week and the other job he worked seven days a week, so the only time I ever saw him was when he was sleeping.

Poor people are the backbone of this country. We fight the wars, we do all the menial work, but the country can't even start thinking about paying a just wage.

It amazes me now when I think about when I first came on welfare. I had no idea about what was going on. I was like a child looking to my caseworker as a god. Whatever she said was law. It just never entered my mind to question anything the worker said. Now I realize all the lies that I've been told. That's the kind of thing you can't forget, but you can work so that it won't happen to other people.

Guaranteed Adequate Income Now

The poverty program is not designed to eliminate poverty. It's used like a pacifier. It hides the true issue. It's really not a help to poor people—it only holds us back. It tries to give us the illusion of having something when in reality we don't. The people who work for the poverty program are the only ones who benefit from it, and they're usually middle-class people, college graduates.

The existing welfare system stinks. There is too much red tape—bureaucracy—too much money goes into the administration of welfare and not enough to the people. Welfare recipients aren't even told their legal rights.

The Welfare Department operates to serve the Welfare Department. Its first interest is not to its clients but to itself. The caseworkers care about themselves and pleasing their supervisors. A lot of times, workers know that clients are being cheated, but instead of going to their supervisor and demanding the recipients' rights, they'll refer them to Welfare Rights. And they're the ones being paid by the government to serve people, but they're too frightened to do that. Usually, the few that try to help are used as an example and fired, or demoted so that they're as good as fired.

And there is a large turnover in caseworkers. Most of them come to the Welfare Department and it's so disgusting that they leave as soon as possible. They leave and think they are doing something good by leaving, but the Welfare Department just brings in another fool to take their place. The caseworkers don't suffer by this—it's the people, the recipients, who suffer. We are kept in a system and are told that it is our fault that we are there, but there really is no way for us to escape.

There are two kinds of welfare. There is welfare for the rich and there is welfare for the poor. Our society couldn't survive without welfare. For the rich, we may change the title and the label, but it's still the same thing—welfare.

Poor people pay taxes—more taxes than rich people do, and all our money is spent just to try to exist, not really live. The poorer you are the more taxes you have to pay and the richer you are the less taxes you have to pay. And it should be the other way around. There are so many tax loopholes, but poor people don't know them like the rich do, and the rich people can hire someone to legally steal for them.

I think there is a need for social services. I think that people should be able to go and request those services, but I don't think that the services should be forced on them. If I feel that I need a psychiatrist, I should have the right to see a psychiatrist. I don't feel that a case-worker has the right to say that a lady needs a psychiatrist. It's a question of really getting down to the problem. People hide the true problems. If your child is hungry or cold, they say he is mentally disturbed, he needs to see a psychiatrist. They don't move toward the cause— we should be feeding and clothing children.

A guaranteed adequate income should replace the present welfare system. People on welfare are treated like we're not a part of this society. There are so many horror stories about people trying to get on welfare that they're beyond telling. People every day coming with no food only to be turned away. People being scared of even coming down and asking for aid, so when they finally do, they're in such bad shape they can't even function.

Especially the elderly. These people work all their lives under the assumption that this makes me dignified, this makes me a person, and when they get to that point in life where our society says they can no longer work they are not properly provided for. That's one of the greatest horrors there is.

Guaranteed Adequate Income Now

A guaranteed adequate income would be a national standard of living that the states couldn't play around with, so they couldn't cheat people. It would make it easier for people to know their rights.

A guaranteed adequate income should replace the poverty program. It would stop people from making money off people just because they're poor. There are many other fields—like the environment—that we haven't explored, that should be dealt with, but people are so busy making money off poor people that they don't have time to do the kind of thing they should be doing to benefit society.

It is very important that we invest in people, in helping people to have a better life, helping our children to have a better education. It takes money to build a better life.

A guaranteed adequate income would put more money into our economy. Poor people spend all their money; we don't have enough to save any. If people had a decent income, they would spend it on better housing, clothes, food, the normal things needed for a decent life.

The business community controls our country and when we don't have good business, we're in trouble. When people don't have buying power, the businesses suffer. A guaranteed adequate income for those who can't work would make a lot of jobs for those who can.

It would also make minimum wages more meaningful. The bulk of our working people are not paid an adequate income, so they should be entitled to some kind of subsidy so that they can have a decent life. This country has a trillion-dollar economy; it is the richest country in the world, and all American people should benefit from it, not just a few. All people contribute to our society in one way or another.

A guaranteed adequate income will recognize work that is not now paid for by society. I think that the greatest thing that a woman can do is to raise her own children, and our society should recognize it as a job. A person should be paid an adequate income to do that.

Finally, a guaranteed adequate income is the best kind of prison reform this country could make, because the way to reform the prisons is to keep people out of them in the first place. Why do poor people go out and commit crimes? Well, if you didn't have a job and couldn't get one and you had to survive somehow, what would you do?

Dignity and justice are things that supposedly are guaranteed to all people in this country, but only a guaranteed adequate income can provide these for most of the people in America today.

Epilogue: What *Will* You Do?

Unfortunately, the people eligible for welfare and not getting it may not read this book. Why? They don't have enough money to buy it.

So the most important thing anyone can do is to get copies of this book into the hands of those people who need it the most.

Here's what you can do:

Buy five more copies of this book and distribute them: for example, one to the next taxi-cab driver you see, one to your maid, one to the next waitress you see, one to a friend, and, if you're a student, one to either the janitor in your dorm or your parents.

This will do two things.

1. Obviously, the more books you buy, the more royalties we'll get—this, in itself, will aid the National Welfare Rights Organization and poor people.

2. And the more people who learn what is in the book, the better. Everyone should learn as much as they can about changing the whole welfare system, so that the people who need welfare will get it, and the people who don't, won't.

While reading a book won't, by itself, help poor people, getting on welfare may. Welfare is not a problem; welfare is the solution to the problem of poverty. Here's what you can do:

Welfare Mothers Speak Out

1. Obtain your state's welfare income scales. These scales show how much a poor family can earn and still be eligible for welfare benefits.

2. Get a list of the wage levels in a particular area.

3. Compare the two in order to find what families are eligible for welfare benefits in addition to their earnings.

4. Inform those families of their right to welfare.

But welfare benefits are not yet high enough to aid all the poor. Here's what you can do:

Call the National Welfare Rights Organization in Washington, D.C. (area code 202, 183-1531) or write us (1424 16th Street, N.W., Washington, D.C. 20036) and we will give you the name and address of the Welfare Rights group in your area of the country so that you may work with poor people in your own hometown to change the welfare laws.

Demand that your legislators tell you how they stand on the welfare issue. Demand that they know the facts. Demand that they vote for *real* welfare reform.

Doesn't it make more sense to have a prosperous economy that is based on providing food, housing, and clothing to *all* the people in the country rather than have a prosperous economy that is based on another war?

What *will* you do?

And if *you* are one of those people who may be eligible for welfare, stop reading this book and go down and apply for it.

Appendices

Appendix A

Farm Subsidy Payments from the Agricultural
Stabilization and Conservation Service,
U.S. Department of Agriculture

Table A.1 Comparison of Payments of $1 Million
or More Received for Participation in ASCS Programs
in One or More of the Following Calendar Years—
1968, 1969, or 1970

State	1968	1969	1970
California			
Fresno County			
Giffin, Inc.	$2,772,187	$3,412,867	$4,095,114
Vista Del Llano Farms	745,647	778,624	1,105,762
Mt. Whitney Farms	—	1,152,294	804,583
Kern County			
H. M. Tenneco	—	—	1,317,051
Kern County Land Co.	780,073	1,080,533	—
Kings County			
J. G. Boswell	3,010,042	4,370,657	4,429,484
South Lake Farms	1,177,320	1,807,697	1,875,454
Salyer Land Co.	786,459	1,637,961	1,547,174
Florida			
Hendry County			
U.S. Sugar Corp.	1,467,498	1,181,195	1,073,980
Hawaii			
Hawaii County			
Hawaiian Com. & Sugar Co.	1,269,021	1,311,225	1,232,166
Waialua Sugar Co., Inc.	530,187	566,785	1,111,060

Appendix B

Major Welfare Programs
(not including cash welfare payments for the poor)

Table B.1 Major Federal Cash Welfare Payments, Fiscal Years 1970 and 1971 (in millions of dollars)

	Cost	
	1970	1971
Program	Actual	Estimated
Agriculture		
Direct payments for commodity purchases	$ 398	$ 316
Feed grain production stabilization	1,644	1,510
Sugar production stabilization	93	84
Wheat production stabilization	863	891
Wool and mohair payments	53	72
Cotton production stabilization	828	918
Conservation related programs	0	0
Medical care		
Health manpower training	226	299
Mental health training and education	120	106
Education and training of health service personnel	90	109
National Institutes of Health training	190	196
Health facilities construction grants	201	170
Health professions facilities construction	146	144
Manpower		
Job-opportunities-in-business sector	221	210
Public service careers	87	94
Manpower development institutional training	321	361
Job Corps	158	160
Neighborhood Youth Corps	315	475
Operation Mainstream	51	72
Concentrated employment program	187	169
Work incentive program	86	71
On-the-job training for veterans	87	164

Appendices

Program	Cost 1970 Actual	Cost 1971 Estimated
Veterans vocational rehabilitation	42	59
Vocational rehabilitation	436	503
Education		
Educational opportunity grants	162	167
Higher education work study	155	164
Science education support	120	101
Veterans educational assistance	939	1,568
Strengthening developing institutions	30	34
Higher educational instructional equipment	0	7
College library resources	10	10
Higher education academic facilities construction	40	43
Foreign language and area studies	15	8
Howard University	57	38
Higher education land-grant colleges and universities	22	13
Institutional support for science	45	35
University community service	9	9
Promotion of the humanities	10	19
Promotion of the arts	12	19
Miscellaneous educational training and fellowships	350	335
International trade		
Export payments on agricultural products	5	5
Export payments	101	166
Housing		
Housing rehabilitation grants	22	38
Farm labor housing grants	2	14
Rent supplement payments	163	0
Specially adapted housing for disabled veterans	8	8
Natural resources		
Rural environmental assistance	185	150
Great plains conservation	15	16
Cropland adjustment program	77	78
Conservation reserve program	37	0
Emergency conservation measures	16	15
Transportation		
Air carrier payments	38	57
Operating differential subsidies	194	224
Construction differential subsidies	68	238
Commerce and economic development		
Community action	365	367
Urban renewal and neighborhood development	1,054	1,035
Model Cities	315	376
Economic development grants	174	160
Appalachian regional development	143	132
Total (in millions of dollars)	$11,801	

Table B.2 Major Welfare Benefits Hidden in the Tax System Fiscal Years 1970 and 1971 (in millions of dollars)

Program	1970 Actual	1971 Estimated
Agriculture		
Expensing and capital gains for farming	$ 880	$ 82
Medical care		
Deductibility of medical expenses	1,700	1,700
Medical insurance premiums and medical care	1,450	1,450
Manpower		
Exclusion of military benefits and allowances	550	500
Education		
Additional exemption for students	525	500
Contributions to educational institutions	200	200
Exclusions of scholarships and fellowships	60	60
International trade		
Western hemisphere trade corporations	55	50
Exclusion of gross-up on dividends of less developed country corporations	55	55
Deferral of foreign subsidiary income	170	165
Exclusion of income earned in U.S. possessions	95	90
Exemption of income earned abroad by U.S. citizens	45	40
Housing		
Deductibility of interest on owner-occupied homes	2,600	2,800
Deductibility of property taxes on owner-occupied homes	2,800	2,900
Exclusion of imputed net rent	0	0
Excess depreciation on rental housing	275	255
Rehabilitation of low-income housing	5	10
Natural resources		
Capital gains treatment for cutting timber	140	130
Expensing of mineral exploration and developing costs	340	325
Excess of percentage over cost depletion	1,470	980
Pollution control amortization	15	15
Capital gains treatment on coal and iron royalties	5	15
Transportation		
Deferral of tax on shipping companies	10	10
Rail freight car amortization	0	105
Commerce and economic development		
Individual dividend exclusion	290	280

Program	Cost 1970 Actual	1971 Estimated
Excess depreciation on buildings	550	500
Investment credit	2,630	910
Corporation capital gains	525	425
Individual capital gains	7,000	7,000
Excess bad debt reserves of financial institutions	680	380
Exemption of credit unions	45	40
Expensing of research and development expenditures	565	540
Corporate surtax exemption	2,300	2,000
Exclusion of interest on life insurance savings	1,050	1,050
Accelerated depreciation revision (ADR)	not available	
Other		
Deductibility of charitable contributions	3,450	3,550
Exemption of interest on state and local debt	2,200	2,300
Exclusion of premiums on group life insurance savings	440	440
Net exclusion of pension contributions for employees	3,150	3,075
Deduction of self-employed pension contributions	160	175
Total (in millions of dollars)	$38,480	$35,840

Table B.3 Major Federal Credit Welfare Programs *
Fiscal 1970
(in millions of dollars)

Program	Gross Outlays	Welfare Costs
Agriculture		
Emergency credit	$ 90	$ 6
Farm operating loans	280	8
Soil and water loans	65	17
Rural electrification loans	362	179
Rural telephone loans	135	67
Storage facility and equipment loans	50	2

* Note:
Government credit welfare occurs in four cases:

    1. When the government loans money at an interest rate below the regular market rate;

    2. When the government guarantees repayment of a loan made in the private sector;

    3. When the government insures a private lender against the default of a loan;

    4. When the government lends money to a person who could not otherwise borrow it.

Table B.3
(*Continued*)

Program	Gross Outlays	Welfare Costs
Price support loans	2,338	87
Farm ownership loans	256	68
Crop insurance	—	9
Medical care		
Health facilities construction loans	—	52
Education		
Higher education facilities loans	102	46
National defense student loans	217	76
College housing	184	84
Law enforcement education aid	18	4
Guaranteed student loans	840	179
Higher education facility interest subsidy	120	45
International trade		
Development loans, revolving fund	560	320
Foreign military credit sales	93	6
Liquidation of foreign military sales fund	44	3
Short-term export credit sales	209	3
Public Law 480	494	226
Export financing—direct loans and participation financing	1,569	65
Housing		
Interest subsidy for homeownership assistance (235)	—	426
Interest subsidy for rental assistance (236)	—	790
Housing opportunity allowance program	—	—
Below market interest range loans on multifamily dwellings [221(d) (3)]	—	69
Rural housing insurance	—	118
Housing for elderly and handicapped	106	53
Rehabilitation fund	39	12
Rural housing direct loans	143	18
Low-rent public housing	—	1,064
Natural resources		
Water and sewer loans	—	22
Commerce and economic development		
Disaster loan fund	91	19
Development company loans	47	6
Small business loans (7a)	84	6
Small business investment company loans	56	1
Economic opportunity loans	35	1
Displaced business loans	31	5

Program	Gross Outlays	Welfare Costs
Economic development-loans for industry	26	2
Economic development-loans for development facilities	15	3
Urban renewal fund	594	16
Total (in millions of dollars)		$4,183

Table B.4 Major Federal Benefit-in-Kind Welfare Programs Fiscal Years 1970 and 1971 (in millions of dollars)

Program	Cost 1970 Actual	1971 Estimated
Food		
School lunch	$ 301	$ 581
School breakfasts	11	15
Nonfood assistance	17	16
Nonschool food program	7	21
Food stamps	551	1,369
School milk program	102	103
Commodity distribution	558	513
Emergency	46	45
Medical care		
Health insurance for the aged (medicare)	1,979	2,070
Medical assistance program (medicaid)	2,638	3,110
Education		
Surplus property utilization	409	426
International trade		
International trade and development policy	19	23
Foreign market development and promotion	15	17
Natural resources		
State and private forestry cooperation	26	28
Resource conservation and development	11	15
Watershed works of improvement	66	78
Rural water and waste disposal systems	45	40
Basic water and sewer facility grants	138	150
Construction grants for wastewater treatment works	426	1,200
Transportation		
Airport development aid program	55	170
The federal airways system [a]	174	174
Urban mass transportation grants	133	270
National rail passenger corporation	0	40

Table B.4
(*Continued*)

Program	Cost 1970 Actual	1971 Estimated
Commerce and economic development		
Postal service	1,510	— a
Government-owned property	—	— a
Sales to domestic ship scrappers	8	— a
Total (in millions of dollars)	$9,245	

a Not estimated.

(Total fiscal 1970 expenditures on major federal welfare programs, not including Public Assistance, Social Security, and the Personal Allowance System amounted to $63 billion.

Direct Cash Payments	$12 billion (approximately)
Benefits Hidden in the Tax System	38 billion
Credit Benefits	4 billion
Benefits-in-Kind	9 billion
Total	$63 billion)

The source of the above tables is U.S. Congress, 92d Cong., 1st sess., Joint Economic Committee Staff Study, *The Economics of Federal Subsidy Programs* (Washington, D.C.: U.S. Government Printing Office, January 11, 1972), pp. 26, 31, 34, 38. This is an intensive discussion of the complete American welfare system.

Appendix C

Aid to Families with Dependent Children

Table C.1 Monthly Amounts for Basic Needs Under Full Standard and Payment Standard and Largest Amount Paid for Basic Needs for a Family Consisting of Four Recipients, by State, July, 1970

State	Monthly Amount for Basic Needs		Largest Amount Paid for Basic Needs [c]	
	Full Standard [a] (standard of need) (1)	Payment Standard [b] (standard of payments) (2)	Amount (3)	Per Cent of Full Standard (column 1) (4)
Alabama	$230	$230	$ 81 [f]	35
Alaska	400	400	375 [f]	94
Arizona	256	256	167 [f]	65

[a] The amount with which income from all sources is compared to determine whether or not financial eligibility exists. Use of the full standard for this purpose (where this is different from the payment standard) is mandatory only for AFDC applicant families with earned income who have not received assistance in any one of the four preceding months.

[b] The amount from which income "available for basic needs" is subtracted to determine the amount of assistance to which a family is entitled. The payment standard cited here is for a family living by itself in rented quarters for which the monthly rental, unless otherwise indicated, is at least as large as the maximum amount allowed by the state for this item.

[c] The total monthly payment for basic needs made under state law or agency regulations to families with no other income.

[d] Data not reported.

[e] These states—twenty-two in all (including the District of Columbia) —have their payment standard below their standard of need.

[f] These nineteen states do not even pay at their standard of payment.

Source: U.S. Department of Health, Education and Welfare, Social and Rehabilitation Service, National Center for Social Statistics, NCSS Report D-2 (July, 1970); OAA and AFDC: Standards for Basic Needs for Specified Types of Assistance Groups, July 1970, Table 4.

Table C.1
(*Continued*)

State	Monthly Amount for Basic Needs		Largest Amount Paid for Basic Needs c	
	Full Standard a (standard of need) (1)	Payment Standard b (standard of payments) (2)	Amount (3)	Per Cent of Full Standard (column 1) (4)
Arkansas	176	176	100 f	57
California	432	432	221 f	51
Colorado	235	235	235	100
Connecticut	330	330	330	100
Delaware	287	236 e	187 f	65
District of Columbia	280	238 e	238	85
Florida	223	223	134 f	60
Georgia	208	208	133 f	64
Guam	— d	— d	— d	— d
Hawaii	263	263	263	100
Idaho	272	242 e	242	89
Illinois	282	282	282	100
Indiana	322	322	150 f	47
Iowa	300	243 e	243	81
Kansas	267	244 e	244	91
Kentucky	264	216 e	187 f	71
Louisiana	213	123	109 f	51
Maine	349	349	168 f	48
Maryland	302	196 e	196	65
Massachusetts	314	314	314	100
Michigan	263	263	263	100
Minnesota	299	299	299	100
Mississippi	232	232	70 f	30
Missouri	325	325	130 f	40
Montana	250	228 e	228	91
Nebraska	330	330	200 f	61
Nevada	317	317	143 f	45
New Hampshire	294	294	294	100
New Jersey	347	347	347	100
New Mexico	203	182 e	182	90
New York	336	336	336	100
North Carolina	184	158 e	158	86
North Dakota	284	261 e	261	92
Ohio	258	200 e	200	78
Oklahoma	218	185 e	185	85
Oregon	281	225 e	225	80
Pennsylvania	313	313	313	100
Puerto Rico	132	132	53 f	40

Appendices

| State | Monthly Amount for Basic Needs | | Largest Amount Paid for Basic Needs [c] | |
	Full Standard [a] (standard of need) (1)	Payment Standard [b] (standard of payments) (2)	Amount (3)	Per Cent of Full Standard (column 1) (4)
Rhode Island	263	263	263	100
South Carolina	198	103 [e]	103	52
Tennessee	217	217	129 [f]	59
Texas	239	179 [e]	179	75
Utah	271	212 [e]	212	78
Vermont	327	304 [e]	304	93
Virgin Islands	— [d]	— [d]	— [d]	— [d]
Virginia	279	261 [e]	261	94
Washington	303	303	303	100
West Virginia	265	138 [e]	138	52
Wisconsin	255	217 [e]	217	85
Wyoming	277	265 [e]	227 [f]	82

Appendix D

Violations of Federal Laws and Regulations in Social and Rehabilitation Service Programs

Table D.1 Violations of Federal Laws and Regulations in Social and Rehabilitation Service Programs by Regions, by State April 1, 1970

State	Total Violations by the States	Assistance Payments Administration									
		Government Reorganization (45 CFR 903.9)	Adjustment of Standards [42 USC 602 (a) (23)]	Deprivation Parental Support (45 CFR 203.1)	Disregard of Income—AFDC [45 CFR 233.20 (a) (4) (iii)]	Durational Residence (45 CFR 202.3)	Foster Care—AFDC (45 CFR 233.10)	Protective Payments (45 CFR 234.60)	Simplified Method Eligibility [45 CFR 205.20 (a)]	Standards of Promptness [HB IV—2200 (B) (3)]	WIN Program (45 CFR 220.35)
Total Violations	535	1	21	12	7	6	4	10	3	3	1
Connecticut	17		I	I	I				I		
Maine	6										

Legend:
    I—No approved plan item for mandatory federal plan requirement
    II—State amendment to approved plan raises question as to compliance with federal requirements
    III—Question raised whether approved plan is followed in practice
    CFR—Code of Federal Regulations
    USC—United States Code

State	Total Violations by the States	Government Reorganization (45 CFR 903.9)	Adjustment of Standards [42 USC 602 (a) (23)]	Deprivation Parental Support (45 CFR 203.1)	Disregard of Income—AFDC [45 CFR 233.20 (a) (4) (iii)]	Durational Residence (45 CFR 202.3)	Foster Care—AFDC (45 CFR 233.10)	Protective Payments (45 CFR 234.60)	Simplified Method Eligibility [45 CFR 205.20 (a)]	Standards of Promptness [HB IV—2200 (B) (3)]	WIN Program (45 CFR 220.35)
					Assistance Payments Administration						
Massachusetts	8										
New Hampshire	9	I	I							I	
Rhode Island	9	I		I							
Vermont	17	I	I								
Delaware	18	I		I					I	III	
New Jersey	9			I	I	I					
New York	18			I				I			
Pennsylvania	21				I	I	I	I	I		
Dist. of Col.	20	I									
Kentucky	3										
Maryland	7	I									
North Carolina	8										
Puerto Rico	16										
Virginia	1										
Virgin Islands	14										

Table D.1
(*Continued*)

State	Total Violations by the States	Government Reorganization (45 CFR 903.9)	Adjustment of Standards [42 USC 602 (a) (23)]	Deprivation Parental Support (45 CFR 203.1)	Disregard of Income—AFDC [45 CFR 233.20 (a) (4) (iii)]	Durational Residence (45 CFR 202.3)	Foster Care—AFDC (45 CFR 233.10)	Protective Payments (45 CFR 234.60)	Simplified Method Eligibility [45 CFR 205.20 (a)]	Standards of Promptness [HB IV—2200 (B) (3)]	WIN Program (45 CFR 220.35)
					Assistance Payments Administration						
West Virginia	0										
Alabama	4										
Florida	6	III									
Georgia	4							I			
Mississippi	6										
South Carolina	3										
Tennessee	8						II				
Illinois	13		I								
Indiana	11		I	I				I		III	
Michigan	16		I					I			
Ohio	9		I								II
Wisconsin	14		I								
Iowa	4						I	I			
Kansas	3		I								

State	Total Violations by the States	Government Reorganization (45 CFR 903.9)	Adjustment of Standards [42 USC 602 (a) (23)]	Deprivation Parental Support (45 CFR 203.1)	Disregard of Income—AFDC [45 CFR 233.20 (a) (4) (iii)]	Durational Residence (45 CFR 202.3)	Foster Care—AFDC (45 CFR 233.10)	Protective Payments (45 CFR 234.60)	Simplified Method Eligibility [45 CFR 205.20 (a)]	Standards of Promptness [HB IV—2200 (B) (3)]	WIN Program (45 CFR 220.35)
										Assistance Payments Administration	
Minnesota	3	I									
Missouri	3									III	
Nebraska	3	I	I								
North Dakota	3			I							
South Dakota	4			I				I			
Arkansas	4										
Louisiana	11							I			
New Mexico	15										
Oklahoma	10										
Texas	14										
Colorado	8	I				I					
Idaho	12	I		I		I					
Montana	10	I									
Utah	15	I						I			
Wyoming	10	I									

Table D.1
(*Continued*)

State · Assistance Payments Administration

	Total Violations by the States	Government Reorganization (45 CFR 903.9)	Adjustment of Standards [42 USC 602 (a) (23)]	Deprivation Parental Support (45 CFR 203.1)	Disregard of Income—AFDC [45 CFR 233.20(a)(4)(iii)]	Durational Residence (45 CFR 202.3)	Foster Care—AFDC (45 CFR 233.10)	Protective Payments (45 CFR 234.60)	Simplified Method Eligibility [45 CFR 205.20(a)]	Standards of Promptness [HB IV—2200(B)(3)]	WIN Program (45 CFR 220.35)
Alaska	7					I					
Arizona	13			I	I	I	III				
California	14	I	I								
Guam	14										
Hawaii	14										
Nevada	16			I							
Oregon	15										
Washington	15										

State	Assistance Payments Administration								
	Confidentiality (HB IV—7000)	Disregard of Income—OAA (45 CFR 233.20)	Disregard of Income—AB (45 CFR 233.20)	Eligibility	Fair Hearings (HB IV—6000)	Intermediate Care (45 CFR 234.130)	Money Payments Unrestricted	Need (45 CFR 213.0)	Single State Agency
Total Violations	2	1	1	9	8	1	1	11	2
Connecticut	II	II	II	II					
Maine									
Massachusetts								II	
New Hampshire									
Rhode Island									
Vermont									
Delaware				III					
New Jersey					II III				
New York					II III			II	
Pennsylvania					II				
Dist. of Col.			II III					II III	
Kentucky									
Maryland					III				

Table D.1
(*Continued*)

State	Confidentiality (HB IV—7000)	Disregard of Income—OAA (45 CFR 233.20)	Disregard of Income—AB (45 CFR 233.20)	Eligibility	Fair Hearings (HB IV—6000)	Intermediate Care (45 CFR 234.130)	Money Payments Unrestricted	Need (45 CFR 213.0)	Single State Agency
North Carolina	II				III				II
Puerto Rico									
Virginia									
Virgin Islands									
West Virginia									
Alabama									
Florida						II		II	III
Georgia									
Mississippi				II				II	
South Carolina									
Tennessee				II				II III	
Illinois							II		
Indiana				III	III				
Michigan									

156

State	Confidentiality (HB IV—7000)	Disregard of Income—OAA (45 CFR 233.20)	Disregard of Income—AB (45 CFR 233.20)	Eligibility	Fair Hearings (HB IV—6000)	Intermediate Care (45 CFR 234.130)	Money Payments Unrestricted	Need (45 CFR 213.0)	Single State Agency
						Assistance Payments Administration			
Ohio									
Wisconsin									
Iowa									
Kansas									
Minnesota									
Missouri									
Nebraska									
North Dakota									
South Dakota									
Arkansas									
Louisiana									
New Mexico									
Oklahoma				II					
Texas									
Colorado									
Idaho									

Table D.1
(*Continued*)

State	Confidentiality (HB IV—7000)	Disregard of Income—OAA (45 CFR 233.20)	Disregard of Income—AB (45 CFR 233.20)	Eligibility	Fair Hearings (HB IV—6000)	Intermediate Care (45 CFR 234.130)	Money Payments Unrestricted	Need (45 CFR 213.0)	Single State Agency
						Assistance Payments Administration			
Montana									
Utah									
Wyoming									
Alaska									
Arizona				II					
California								II	
Guam									
Hawaii								II III	
Nevada									
Oregon									
Washington									

State	Community Services Administration									
	Entire Plan (45 CFR Part 220)	Single Organizational Unit (45 CFR 220.2)	Advisory Committees (45 CFR 220.4)	Use of Professional Staff (45 CFR 220.5)	Use of Subprofessional Personnel (45 CFR 220.6)	Use of Volunteers (45 CFR 220.7)	Staff Development (45 CFR 220.10)	Child Care Services (45 CFR 220.18)	Births out of Wedlock (45 CFR 220.20)	Family Planning Services (45 CFR 220.21)
Total Violations	2	4	7	1	1	1	1	1	1	1
Connecticut										
Maine										
Massachusetts										
New Hampshire										
Rhode Island										
Vermont		I								
Delaware										
New Jersey										
New York										
Pennsylvania	I	I								
Dist. of Col.		III								
Kentucky			III							
Maryland										
North Carolina			III							
Puerto Rico										

159

Table D.1
(*Continued*)

State	Entire Plan (45 CFR Part 220)	Single Organizational Unit (45 CFR 220.2)	Advisory Committees (45 CFR 220.4)	Use of Professional Staff (45 CFR 220.5)	Use of Subprofessional Personnel (45 CFR 220.6)	Use of Volunteers (45 CFR 220.7)	Staff Development (45 CFR 220.10)	Child Care Services (45 CFR 220.18)	Births out of Wedlock (45 CFR 220.20)	Family Planning Services (45 CFR 220.21)
Virginia										
Virgin Islands			III						III	III
West Virginia										
Alabama										
Florida										
Georgia										
Mississippi										
South Carolina										
Tennessee										
Illinois		III								
Indiana										
Michigan										
Ohio		III								
Wisconsin										

State — Community Services Administration

Appendices

State	Community Services Administration									
	Entire Plan (45 CFR Part 220)	Single Organizational Unit (45 CFR 220.2)	Advisory Committees (45 CFR 220.4)	Use of Professional Staff (45 CFR 220.5)	Use of Subprofessional Personnel (45 CFR 220.6)	Use of Volunteers (45 CFR 220.7)	Staff Development (45 CFR 220.10)	Child Care Services (45 CFR 220.18)	Births out of Wedlock (45 CFR 220.20)	Family Planning Services (45 CFR 220.21)
Iowa										
Kansas										
Minnesota										
Missouri										
Nebraska										
North Dakota										
South Dakota										
Arkansas										
Louisiana										
New Mexico										
Oklahoma										
Texas										
Colorado										
Idaho								III		
Montana		III								
Utah			III	III	III	III	III			

Table D.1
(*Continued*)

State   Community Services Administration

	Entire Plan (45 CFR Part 220)	Single Organizational Unit (45 CFR 220.2)	Advisory Committees (45 CFR 220.4)	Use of Professional Staff (45 CFR 220.5)	Use of Subprofessional Personnel (45 CFR 220.6)	Use of Volunteers (45 CFR 220.7)	Staff Development (45 CFR 220.10)	Child Care Services (45 CFR 220.18)	Births out of Wedlock (45 CFR 220.20)	Family Planning Services (45 CFR 220.21)
Wyoming										
Alaska										
Arizona	I		I							
California										
Guam										
Hawaii										
Nevada										
Oregon										
Washington										

Appendices

State	Community Services Administration			State	Community Services Administration		
	Child Welfare Services (45 CFR 220.40)	Implementation (45 CFR 220.47)	Single State Agency [45 CFR 220.49 (a) (1) (ii)]		Child Welfare Services (45 CFR 220.40)	Implementation (45 CFR 220.47)	Single State Agency [45 CFR 220.49 (a) (1) (ii)]
Total Violations	1	1	1	Total Violations	1	1	1
Connecticut				North Carolina			
Maine				Puerto Rico			
Massachusetts				Virginia			
New Hampshire				Virgin Islands			
Rhode Island				West Virginia			
Vermont				Alabama			
Delaware				Florida			III
New Jersey				Georgia			
New York				Mississippi			
Pennsylvania		I		South Carolina			
Dist. of Col.				Tennessee			
Kentucky				Illinois			
Maryland				Indiana			

Table D.1
(*Continued*)

State	Community Services Administration			State	Community Services Administration		
	Child Welfare Services (45 CFR 220.40)	Implementation (45 CFR 220.47)	Single State Agency [45 CFR 220.49 (a) (1) (ii)]		Child Welfare Services (45 CFR 220.40)	Implementation (45 CFR 220.47)	Single State Agency [45 CFR 220.49 (a) (1) (ii)]
Michigan				Texas			
Ohio				Colorado			
Wisconsin				Idaho			
Iowa				Montana			
Kansas				Utah	III		
Minnesota				Wyoming			
Missouri				Alaska			
Nebraska				Arizona			
North Dakota				California			
South Dakota				Guam			
Arkansas				Hawaii			
Louisiana				Nevada			
New Mexico				Oregon			
Oklahoma				Washington			

State	State Financial Participation 45 CFR 250.240—P.R.40-2	Third-Party Payments 45 CFR 250.31—P.R. 40-3	Reasonable Charges 45 CFR 250.30—P.R. 40-4	Utilization Review 45 CFR 250.20—P.R. 40-9	Early Screening, Diagnosis 45 CFR 249.10—P.R.40-11	Standards of Skilled Nursing Homes 45 CFR 249.33—P.R. 40-12	Provider Agreements 45 CFR 250.21—P.R. 40-13	Free Choice of Provider 1902 (a) (23)	Provision for Consultative Services 1902 (a) (24)
					Medical Services Administration				
Total Violations	1	9	23	13	24	23	23	25	23
Connecticut		I	I						
Maine									
Massachusetts									
New Hampshire			I						
Rhode Island			III					I	
Vermont			I		I	I	I	I	I
Delaware		I	I	I	I	I	I	I	I
New Jersey									
New York			I		I	I	I	I	I
Pennsylvania	I		I		I			I	I
Dist. of Col.		I	I	I	I	I	I	I	I
Kentucky									
Maryland			I						
North Carolina									

Table D.1
(*Continued*)

State   Medical Services Administration

State	State Financial Participation 45 CFR 250.240—P.R.40-2	Third-Party Payments 45 CFR 250.31—P.R. 40-3	Reasonable Charges 45 CFR 250.30—P.R. 40-4	Utilization Review 45 CFR 250.20—P.R. 40-9	Early Screening, Diagnosis 45 CFR 249.10—P.R.40-11	Standards of Skilled Nursing Homes 45 CFR 249.33—P.R. 40-12	Provider Agreements 45 CFR 250.21—P.R. 40-13	Free Choice of Provider 1902 (a) (23)	Provision for Consultative Services 1902 (a) (24)
Puerto Rico		I	I	I	I	I	I	I	I
Virginia									
Virgin Islands						I	I		I
West Virginia									
Alabama									
Florida									
Georgia					I	I			
Mississippi									
South Carolina		III							
Tennessee									
Illinois					I	I	I	I	
Indiana									
Michigan		I	I	I	I	I	I		I

State — Medical Services Administration

State	State Financial Participation 45 CFR 250.240—P.R.40-2	Third-Party Payments 45 CFR 250.31—P.R. 40-3	Reasonable Charges 45 CFR 250.30—P.R. 40-4	Utilization Review 45 CFR 250.20—P.R. 40-9	Early Screening, Diagnosis 45 CFR 249.10—P.R.40-11	Standards of Skilled Nursing Homes 45 CFR 249.33—P.R. 40-12	Provider Agreements 45 CFR 250.21—P.R. 40-13	Free Choice of Provider 1902 (a) (23)	Provision for Consultative Services 1902 (a) (24)
Ohio									
Wisconsin		I	I	I	I	III		I	I
Iowa									
Kansas									
Minnesota									
Missouri									
Nebraska									
North Dakota									
South Dakota									
Arkansas									
Louisiana					I	I	I	I	I
New Mexico	I	I	I	I	I	I		I	I
Oklahoma		I	I	I	I			I	I
Texas	I	I	I	I			I	I	I
Colorado					I		I	I	I

Appendices

Table D.1
(*Continued*)

State	Medical Services Administration								
	State Financial Participation 45 CFR 250.240—P.R.40-2	Third-Party Payments 45 CFR 250.31—P.R. 40-3	Reasonable Charges 45 CFR 250.30—P.R. 40-4	Utilization Review 45 CFR 250.20—P.R. 40-9	Early Screening, Diagnosis 45 CFR 249.10—P.R.40-11	Standards of Skilled Nursing Homes 45 CFR 249.33—P.R. 40-12	Provider Agreements 45 CFR 250.21—P.R. 40-13	Free Choice of Provider 1902 (a) (23)	Provision for Consultative Services 1902 (a) (24)
Idaho		I			I	I	I	I	I
Montana					I	I	I	I	I
Utah					I	I	I	I	I
Wyoming		I			I	I	I	I	I
Alaska									
Arizona									
California		I	I	I	I	I	I	I	I
Guam	I	I	I	I			I	I	
Hawaii					I	I	I	I	I
Nevada	I	I	I	I	I	I	I	I	I
Oregon		I	I	I	I	I	I	I	I
Washington	I	I	I	I	I	I	I	I	I

State	Medical Services Administration					
	Medical Review 1902 (a) (26)	Agreements Under Title V 1902 (a) (11) (B)	Staffing for Provisions of Mental Health H.B. D-7300	Staffing Medical Assistance Unit H.B. D-7200	Modification Comparability 45 CFR 249.41	Amt., Duration, & Scope of Medical Assistance 45 CFR 249.10 (a) (4) (6)
Total Violations	29	36	5	3	1	1
Connecticut			III			
Maine						
Massachusetts	I	I				
New Hampshire						
Rhode Island						
Vermont	I	I	III			
Delaware	I	I	III	III	I	
New Jersey						
New York	I	I				
Pennsylvania		I	III			III
Dist. of Col.	I	I				
Kentucky		I				

Table D.1
(*Continued*)

State	Medical Review 1902 (a) (26)	Agreements Under Title V 1902 (a) (11) (B)	Staffing for Provisions of Mental Health H.B. D-7300	Staffing Medical Assistance Unit H.B. D-7200	Modification Comparability 45 CFR 249.41	Amt., Duration, & Scope of Medical Assistance 45 CFR 249.10 (a) (4) (6)
			Medical Services Administration			
Maryland						
North Carolina						
Puerto Rico	I	I				
Virginia						
Virgin Islands	I	I				
West Virginia						
Alabama						
Florida						
Georgia		I				
Mississippi						
South Carolina			III	III		

Appendices

State	Medical Services Administration					
	Medical Review 1902 (a) (26)	Agreements Under Title V 1902 (a) (11) (B)	Staffing for Provisions of Mental Health H.B. D-7300	Staffing Medical Assistance Unit H.B. D-7200	Modification Comparability 45 CFR 249.41	Amt., Duration, & Scope of Medical Assistance 45 CFR 249.10 (a) (4) (6)
Tennessee						
Illinois		I				
Indiana				III		
Michigan	I	I				
Ohio		I				
Wisconsin	I	I				
Iowa	I	I				
Kansas	I	I				
Minnesota	I	I				
Missouri	I	I				
Nebraska		I				
North Dakota	I	I				
South Dakota	I	I				

Table D.1
(*Continued*)

State	Medical Services Administration					
	Medical Review 1902 (a) (26)	Agreements Under Title V 1902 (a) (11) (B)	Staffing for Provisions of Mental Health H.B. D-7300	Staffing Medical Assistance Unit H.B. D-7200	Modification Comparability 45 CFR 249.41	Amt., Duration, & Scope of Medical Assistance 45 CFR 249.10 (a) (4) (6)
Arkansas						
Louisiana		I				
New Mexico	I	I				
Oklahoma	I	I				
Texas	I	I				
Colorado	I	I				
Idaho	I	I				
Montana	I	I				
Utah	I	I				
Wyoming	I	I				
Alaska						

State	Medical Review 1902 (a) (26)	Agreements Under Title V 1902 (a) (11) (B)	Staffing for Provisions of Mental Health H.B. D-7300	Staffing Medical Assistance Unit H.B. D-7200	Modification Comparability 45 CFR 249.41	Amt., Duration, & Scope of Medical Assistance 45 CFR 249.10 (a) (4) (6)
	Medical Services Administration					
Arizona						
California	I	I				
Guam	I	I				
Hawaii	I	I				
Nevada	I	I				
Oregon	I	I				
Washington	I	I				

Table D.1
(*Continued*)

State	Office of Research Demonstration and Training		Rehabilitation and Services Administration					
	Subprofessional & Volunteers (45 CFR 225)	Staff Development (HBPA III 3200.3 a & b)	Follow-up Services (45 CFR 40.141 and 401.50)	Def. of Dis. Beneficiary [45 CFR 401.113 (a)]	Program Planning (45 CFR 401.15)	Program Evaluation (45 CFR 401.15)	Residence Prohibition (45 CFR 40.130)	New State Plan
Total Violations	8	1	34	34	34	34	16	9
Connecticut	I		I	I	I	I	I	
Maine			I	I	I	I	I	I
Massachusetts			I	I	I	I	I	
New Hampshire			I	I	I	I	I	
Rhode Island			I	I	I	I	I	
Vermont			I	I	I	I	I	
Delaware	I							
New Jersey			I	I	I	I		
New York	III		I	I	I	I		
Pennsylvania			I	I	I	I		
Dist. of Col.			I	I	I	I		
Kentucky				I				

Appendices

State	Office of Research Demonstration and Training		Rehabilitation and Services Administration					New State Plan
	Subprofessional & Volunteers (45 CFR 225)	Staff Development (HBPA III 3200.3 a & b)	Follow-up Services (45 CFR 40.141 and 401.50)	Def. of Dis. Beneficiary [45 CFR 401.113 (a)]	Program Planning (45 CFR 401.15)	Program Evaluation (45 CFR 401.15)	Residence Prohibition (45 CFR 40.130)	
Maryland			I	I	I	I		
North Carolina			I	I	I	I		
Puerto Rico			I	I	I	I	I	I
Virginia			I					
Virgin Islands			I	I	I	I	I	I
West Virginia								
Alabama			I	I	I	I		
Florida								II
Georgia								
Mississippi			I	I	I	I		
South Carolina								
Tennessee			I	I	I	I		
Illinois			I	I	I	I	I	
Indiana			I	I	I	I		

Table D.1
(*Continued*)

State	Office of Research Demonstration and Training		Rehabilitation and Services Administration					
	Subprofessional & Volunteers (45 CFR 225)	Staff Development (HBPA III 3200.3 a & b)	Follow-up Services (45 CFR 40.141 and 401.50)	Def. of Dis. Beneficiary [45 CFR 401.113 (a)]	Program Planning (45 CFR 401.15)	Program Evaluation (45 CFR 401.15)	Residence Prohibition (45 CFR 40.130)	New State Plan
Michigan			I	I	I	I	I	
Ohio			I	I	I	I	I	
Wisconsin			I	I	I	I		
Iowa								
Kansas								
Minnesota								
Missouri								
Nebraska								
North Dakota								
South Dakota								
Arkansas			I	I	I	I		
Louisiana			I	I	I	I		
New Mexico			I	I	I	I		I
Oklahoma								I

State	Office of Research Demonstration and Training		Rehabilitation and Services Administration					
	Subprofessional & Volunteers (45 CFR 225)	Staff Development (HBPA III 3200.3 a & b)	Follow-up Services (45 CFR 40.141 and 401.50)	Def. of Dis. Beneficiary [45 CFR 401.113 (a)]	Program Planning (45 CFR 401.15)	Program Evaluation (45 CFR 401.15)	Residence Prohibition (45 CFR 40.130)	New State Plan
Texas			I	I	I	I		I
Colorado								
Idaho								
Montana	I							
Utah								
Wyoming	I							
Alaska	I		I	I	I	I	I	
Arizona		III	I	I	I	I	I	
California					I	I		
Guam	I		I	I	I	I	I	
Hawaii	I		I	I	I	I		
Nevada			I	I	I	I		I
Oregon			I	I	I	I	I	I
Washington			I	I	I	I	I	

Appendix E

An Explanation of the Bill of Welfare Rights

It is important for every welfare recipient to know what his or her rights are. It is just as important to know where those rights come from. This is important so that the recipient can tell the Welfare Department why it is wrong and so that he or she can tell other people—such as other people in Welfare Rights, people from the press, and others who can help—why the recipient's position is right and the Welfare Department's decision is wrong.

1. *Everyone has the right to apply for any welfare program and to have that application put in writing.* The Federal Handbook of Public Assistance Administration, Part IV, Section 22, and the Social Security Act, 42 USC 602, guarantee the right of any person to make an application for aid, put it in writing, or have the assistance of a welfare worker in putting the application in writing. Once a request for aid has been made, it is the responsibility of the Welfare Department to put the application in writing. No discouragement by welfare workers can change the fact that an application has been made.

2. *Everyone has the right to have the Welfare Department make a decision promptly after the application for aid.* The Federal Handbook of Public Assistance Administration, Part IV, Section 2200, requires that prompt action is to be taken on every application for welfare. This means that the Welfare Department can take *no longer than thirty days* to make its decision whether to give aid or

reject giving aid. If the decision is to give aid, assistance has to be provided promptly after the decision. If the Welfare Department takes too long, one has the right to request a fair hearing immediately.

3. *Everyone has the right to be told in writing the specific reason for any denial of aid.* The Federal Handbook of Public Assistance Administration, Part IV, Section 2200, requires that an application for aid cannot be rejected by the Welfare Department worker's simply telling the applicant that he or she is not eligible. The applicant must be given not only written notice of the rejection but also written notice *of the specific reason for the rejection.* The purpose of this right is to make it possible to show that the reason is wrong, whether because the department's rule or policy is mistakenly applied in the case or because no such rule or policy is permissible (the applicant couldn't show that the reason was wrong if he or she wasn't even told why the application was rejected).

4. *Everyone has the right to appeal a denial of aid and to be given a fair hearing before an impartial referee.* The Social Security Act, 42 USC 602 states that a basic right of persons receiving and applying for aid is the right to object to the decision of the Welfare Department and to be given a fair hearing in review of that decision. Fair-hearing complaints often concern:

  denial of aid or cutting off of aid;

  too little money in the welfare grant;

  failure of the Welfare Department to act on a request within thirty days;

  "vendor payments"—when the Welfare Department pays money directly to a person's landlord or other creditor instead of to the recipient;

giving aid on the condition that a recipient does work; and

any action by the Welfare Department in which a recipient feels that fair treatment has not been given.

Fair hearings are not meant to be rubber stamps of the County Welfare Department's action. They are conducted by a representative of the State Welfare Department and decided by the State Board of Public Welfare. The law requires that the hearing officer, the person conducting the hearing, be impartial and be someone who has not been involved in the County Welfare Department's decision against which the appeal has been taken. All persons who request a fair hearing have the following rights:

the right to be represented or accompanied and advised by any person (whether a lawyer or not);

the right to bring witnesses and to cross-examine the Welfare Department's witnesses;

the right to present ideas in a convenient and informal way;

the right to have the hearing held at a place reasonably near the applicant's home. Or, if this proves impossible, the right to have transportation provided to the hearing place (for both the applicant and witnesses);

the right to have the hearing decision made *promptly*— this means that final administrative action must be taken within *sixty days* from the date of the request for a fair hearing; and

the right to get retroactive payments if you win the hearing (from the date of the wrongful decision)

5. *All welfare recipients have the right to a hearing before their checks can be reduced or cut off and before medical aid is affected.* The Supreme Court has said (in *Goldberg v. Kelly* 397 U.S. 254, 1970) that, under the United States Constitution's Fourteenth Amendment, a person receiving

aid has the right to a hearing before the person's check can be cut or reduced or his medical care benefits changed. Under the Court's decision and federal regulations (CFR sec. 205.10), this right means that, whenever the Welfare Department takes action cutting or reducing a person's aid, the person must be told:

that he has the right to a fair hearing;

how to obtain a fair hearing;

that the person may be represented by a lawyer, relative, friend, or Welfare Rights worker; and

whether or not the state will pay legal fees for people requesting fair hearings

Remember, aid must continue until a fair-hearing decision is made. Recipients cannot be cut off until then. This case was brought to court and won by the Welfare Rights Organization in New York and Nevada, but it applies to all recipients in the country.

6. *All applicants and recipients have the right to fair and equal treatment, free from discrimination based on race, color, or religion* (sex or hair length, etc.). The First and Fourteenth Amendments to the United States Constitution guarantee that all citizens are supposed to be treated equally, and not discriminated against on the basis of race, color, or religion, or any other factor. Different amounts of grants cannot be given to welfare recipients because of race; nor can welfare rooms or other facilities be segregated; nor can black welfare recipients be treated discourteously. Welfare recipients also have the right to insist that welfare caseworkers be hired in a way which does not discriminate and which assures that the welfare staff is completely integrated.

7. *All welfare recipients have the right to get welfare payments without being forced to spend the money as the Welfare Department wants.* The Federal Handbook of

Assistance Administration, Part IV, Section 5100,
es that the welfare recipient is to be given his or her
aid in the form of money (either cash or check). The purpose of this requirement is to enable the recipient to
spend the money as he or she wants. The Welfare Department cannot tell the recipient how to spend his or
her money; welfare recipients have the right to spend their
money how and when they see fit.

8. *All applicants and recipients have the right to be treated
with respect.* Like all other citizens, welfare recipients
have the right to be treated with respect by the employees
of their government. Welfare recipients have the right to
courteous and respectful treatment by all employees of
the Welfare Department. Welfare Department employees
should always use the courtesy title (Miss, Mrs., Ms., or
Mr.) when they address the applicant or recipient.

9. *All applicants and recipients have the right to be treated
in a way which does not invade a person's right to privacy.*
The Fourth Amendment to the United States Constitution
protects all citizens from unlawful searches, thereby assuring the right to privacy. This means that welfare recipients
can refuse to let investigators into their house at any time
without jeopardizing their welfare assistance, except in a
case where a child is being mistreated, as the Supreme
Court has ruled. Welfare workers should not visit recipients' homes at inconvenient times such as at night, during
holidays, or on Sundays. They can be forced to make sure
that they do not come by the houses except at agreeable
times. No welfare investigator or social worker can search
a recipient's home without his or her permission or without
a search warrant, or remove anything from the recipient's
home without permission.

182

10. *All welfare recipients have the right to receive welfare aid without having the Welfare Department ask questions about who their social friends are (such as who they are going out with).* Under the United States Supreme Court Case *Smith* v. *King,* 392 U.S. 309, 1968, and under new regulations passed by HEW, the Welfare Department cannot deny, cut off, or reduce welfare aid because a recipient is going out with someone. A welfare recipient has an absolute right to date anyone he or she wants to without having the welfare aid affected. This means that welfare workers cannot snoop around and ask questions about a recipient's social life that he or she does not want to answer. These matters are none of the social worker's business.

11. *All welfare recipients have the right to have the same constitutional protections all other citizens have.* A welfare recipient cannot be made to give up or limit any constitutional rights because he or she is on welfare. This means that recipients have the same rights to speak, practice religion, organize people into groups or help in campaigns, refuse to make statements that will hurt them during criminal investigations, refuse to let policemen search their homes or unlawfully arrest them, and all the other rights that people not on welfare have.

12. *All welfare recipients have the right to be told and informed by the Welfare Department of all of their rights, including the ways they can best make sure that they can get their welfare money.* The Federal Handbook of Public Assistance Administration, Part IV, Section 2200, requires that the Welfare Department tell welfare recipients and applicants how they may show that they are eligible, of their right to a fair hearing, of their rights in the hearing (when they request it), of their right to make an applica-

tion in writing and get their aid promptly or get a notice of the reasons for rejection, and of their right to equal treatment without regard to race or color or other factors. All other rights should be explained as well.

13. *Everyone has the right to have, to get, and to give advice during all contacts with the Welfare Department, including when applying, when being investigated, and during fair hearings.* Welfare recipients have the right to be accompanied by a lawyer, advocate, or member of a Welfare Rights Organization during all contacts with the Welfare Department, including application, administrative reviews, investigations, and fair hearings. Welfare recipients also have the right to represent their fellow recipients.

14. *Everyone has the right to be a member of a Welfare Rights Organization.* The First Amendment to the United States Constitution guarantees to *all* citizens the right of freedom of association. This means that welfare recipients, like all other citizens, have the right to participate in private organizations of their own choosing. Welfare recipients have the right to be members and leaders of a Welfare Rights Organization, civil rights group, or any other organization they want to be in. *It is against the law for the Welfare Department to take any action against a welfare recipient because of his or her participation in these organizations.*

Notes

Chapter 1

1. Herbert J. Gans, "Three Ways to Solve the Welfare Problem," *The New York Times* Magazine, March 7, 1971, p. 100.
2. John S. Lang, *The Washington Post*, October 5, 1969, pp. A1, A7.
3. Nick Kotz, "Rich Farmers Split Holdings to Save Subsidies," *The Washington Post*, July 5, 1971, p. A1.
4. U.S. Senator Birch Bayh, as reported in *The New York Times*, July 15, 1971, p. 31.
5. Kotz, "Rich Farmers." See also U.S. Bureau of the Budget, February, 1970.
6. U.S. Representative Henry Reuss, as reported in *The Milwaukee Journal*, March 29, 1971, p. 13.
7. *The New York Times*, May 5, 1971, p. 53. See also *The New York Times*, May 9, 1971, p. 41.
8. *The New York Times*, October 22, 1970, pp. 1, 34; *The New York Times*, December 31, 1970, p. 24; *The New York Times*, December 13, 1970, p. 1; *The New York Times*, August 3, 1971, pp. 1, 39.
9. Walter Heller, as reported in *The New York Times*, August 20, 1971, p. 42.
10. Gaylord Shaw, Associated Press Study of Federal Subsidy Programs, as reported in *The Milwaukee Journal*, August 1, 1971, p. 3. See also U.S. Congress, Joint Economic Committee, staff study, *The Economics of Federal Subsidy Programs*, 92d Cong., 1st sess. (Washington, D.C.: U.S. Government Printing Office, January 11, 1972).
11. U.S., Department of Commerce, Bureau of the Census, *Statistical Abstract of the United States, 1970*, 91st ed. (Washington, D.C.: U.S. Government Printing Office, 1970), p. 277. See also, *The Milwaukee Journal*, June 7, 1971, p. 18.

Chapter 3

1. Tom Wolfe, *Radical Chic and Mau-Mauing the Flak Catchers* (New York: Farrar, Straus, and Giroux, 1970). Also, Richard W. Poston, *The Gang and the Establishment* (New York: Harper and Row, 1971). More importantly, see Frances Fox Piven and Richard A. Cloward, *Regulating*

the Poor: The Functions of Public Welfare (New York: Pantheon, 1971).

2. *The New York Times,* November 8, 1970, p. 54.

3. *Ibid.*

4. *Ibid.*

5. *Ibid.*

6. *Ibid.*

7. *Ibid.*

8. Jack Anderson, "Millions for Poor Sidetracked," *The Washington Post,* October 22, 1970, p. B7.

9. *Ibid.*

10. *Ibid.*

11. Jack Anderson, "Getting Rich Off Poverty," *The Washington Post,* October 25, 1970, p. B7.

12. *Ibid.*

13. *Ibid.*

14. Cited in Anderson, "Millions for Poor Sidetracked."

15. Dennis Chapman, unpublished letter to the editor of *The Washington Post,* dated October 27, 1970.

16. *The New York Times,* Nov. 8, 1970, p. 54.

17. Samuel F. Yette, *The Choice: The Issue of Black Survival in America* (New York: G. P. Putnam's Sons, 1971), p. 44.

18. *Ibid.,* p. 45.

19. *The Milwaukee Sentinel,* March 13, 1971, p. 12.

20. *Ibid.*

21. U.S. Congress, Senate, Subcommittee on Employment, Manpower, and Poverty, of the Committee on Labor and Public Welfare, *The JOBS Program—Background Information,* 91st Cong., 2d sess, April, 1970, p. 132.

22. *The Milwaukee Sentinel,* March 13, 1971, p. 12.

23. *The Milwaukee Sentinel,* May 2, 1971, pp. 1, 10.

Chapter 5

1. Most of this can be found in 42 United States Code 602. The rest is referred to in Appendix D of this book.

2. Stephen Clapp, "Welfare Chiselers," *Public Information Center News,* I, 6 (1970), 2.

3. *The New York Times,* March 21, 1971, p. 38.

4. Ronald Reagan, "Welfare Is a Cancer," *The New York Times,* April 1, 1971, p. 41.

5. *The Milwaukee Journal,* April 3, 1971, p. 3.

6. U.S., Congress, Senate, Hon. Meade Whitaker, *Hearings Before the Committee on Finance,* 91st Cong., 2nd sess., September 21, 1970, Part 2, pp. 784–92.

Chapter 8

1. U.S., Department of Health, Education and Welfare (HEW), *Estimated Employability of Recipients of Public Assistance Money Payments,* July, 1968.

2. Stephen F. Gold, "The Failure of the Work Incentive Program," *The University of Pennsylvania Law Review,* vol. 119, no. 3, p. 495.

3. *The New York Times,* March 23, 1971, p. 75.

4. Samuel F. Yette, *The Choice: The Issue of Black Survival in America* (New York: G. P. Putnam's Sons, 1971), p. 48. See also, *The New York Times,* March 3, 1971, p. 1.

5. *The New York Times,* March 3, 1971, p. 46.

6. President's Commission on Income Maintenance Programs, Ben W. Heineman, Chairman, *Poverty Amid Plenty: The American Paradox* (Washington, D.C.: U.S. Government Printing Office, 1969), p. 74.

7. Day Care and Child Development Council of America, "Components and Annual Operating Costs Per Child for the Three Major Kinds of Day Care Facilities, 1970."

8. U.S., HEW, Social and Rehabilitation Service (SRS), National Center for Social Statistics (NCSS), *Findings of the 1967 AFDC Study: Data by State and Census Division,* July, 1970, table 40.

9. U.S., HEW, SRS, Office of Research, Demonstrations, and Training, *Welfare Policy and Its Consequences for the Recipient Population: A Study of the AFDC Program* (Washington, D.C.: U.S. Government Printing Office, 1969), p. xvii.

10. U.S., Department of Commerce, Bureau of the Census, *Income Growth Rates,* P-60, April 6, 1970, table A-3.

11. U.S., HEW, *Preliminary Report of the 1969 AFDC Study,* NCSS Report AFDC-1 (69), March, 1970, table 38.

12. Charles McCabe, "Get 'Em off Welfare," *The San Francisco Chronicle,* April 26, 1971, p. 35.

13. *The New York Times,* October 4, 1971, pp. 1, 77. See also *The New York Times,* October 12, 1971, p. 34.

14. New York Urban Coalition, "The Working Poor—the Problem of Low-Wage Workers in New York City," September, 1970, p. 11. See also, *The New York Times,* September 22, 1970, p. 1.

15. Unpublished statistics obtained from HEW, Assistance Payments Administration, Public Information Office, 1970.

16. Frances Fox Piven, and Richard A. Cloward, *Regulating the Poor: The Functions of Public Relief* (New York: Pantheon, 1971), pp. 215, 218.

17. U.S., HEW, SRS, NCSS, *Public Assistance Statistics, December, 1970,* table 7.

Notes

18. James C. Vadakin, *Family Allowances* (Miami, Fla.: University of Miami Press, 1958), p. 18.

19. Jeffry Galper, "The Speenhamland Scales: Political, Social, or Economic Disaster?" *The Social Service Review*, XLIV, 1 (March, 1970), p. 61.

20. Mark Blaug, "The Myth of the Old Poor Law," *Journal of Economic History*, XXIII (1963), 174.

21. *Ibid.*, p. 173.

22. Mark Blaug, "The Poor Law Report Revisited," *Journal of Economic History*, XXIV (June, 1964), 229.

23. *Ibid.*, p. 231. See also, Galper, "The Speenhamland Scales," p. 59.

24. HEW study reported in *The Boston Globe*, April 18, 1970, p. 10.

25. *The New York Times*, November 30, 1969, p. 60.

26. *The Milwaukee Journal*, February 12, 1971, p. 2.

27. U.S., HEW, SRS, NCSS, *Public Assistance Statistics, December, 1970*, p. 7.

28. *The Milwaukee Journal*, June 4, 1971, p. 4.

29. *The New York Times*, January 10, 1971, p. 35.

30. U.S., Department of Labor, Bureau of Labor Statistics, *Spring 1970 Cost Estimates for Urban Family Budgets*, December 21, 1970, p. 1.

31. Philip M. Stern, *The Great Treasury Raid* (New York: Random House, 1964), p. 162.

32. U.S., HEW, SRS, *Report on the Disposition of Public Assistance Cases (Federally Funded Programs) Involving Questions of Fraud, Fiscal Year 1970*, p. 1.

33. Herbert J. Gans, "Three Ways to Solve the Welfare Problem," *The New York Times* Magazine, March 7, 1971, p. 94.

34. "Does the Declaration System Really Work?" *Welfarer*, I (September, 1969), 2. See also, The Center on Social Welfare Policy and Law, Columbia University, *H. R. 1: The Opportunities for Families Program and Family Assistance Plan*, May, 1971, p. 37.

35. *The Milwaukee Journal*, February 7, 1971, p. 18.

36. U.S., HEW, SRS, NCSS, Program Statistics and Data Services, *Source of Funds Expended for Public Assistance Payments, for the Cost of Administration, Services, and Training: Fiscal Year Ended June 30, 1970*, table 2.

37. U.S. Bureau of the Budget, February, 1970.

38. U.S., HEW, *Source of Funds Expended*.

39. U.S., HEW, SRS, NCSS, *Public Assistance Statistics, January 1971*, p. 6. See also, *The Milwaukee Journal*, June 6, 1971, p. 18.

Notes

Chapter 9

1. This and the following usage of tax exemptions and deductions for a family of four, and for elderly and middle-aged couples, is based in the U.S. federal income tax which was in effect until 1970. Most recent tax changes have increased the personal exemption to $750.

2. George H. Hildebrand, *Poverty, Income Maintenance, and the Negative Income Tax* (Ithaca: New York State School of Industrial and Labor Relations, Cornell University, 1967), p. 23.

3. Milton Friedman, *Capitalism and Freedom* (Chicago: Phoenix Books, University of Chicago Press, 1963), pp. 190–92.

4. Hildebrand, *Poverty, Income Maintenance*, pp. 31–36.

5. James Tobin, "The Case for an Income Guarantee," *The Public Interest*, No. 4, Summer, 1966, pp. 31–41.

6. Ripon Society, "The Negative Income Tax," *The Ripon Forum*, III, 4 (April, 1967), p. 6.

7. The President's Commission on Income Maintenance Programs, *Poverty Amid Plenty: The American Paradox* (Washington, D.C.: U.S. Government Printing Office, 1969), pp. 57–58.

8. *Ibid.*, p. 7.

9. Robert Theobald, *Free Men and Free Markets* (New York: Clarkson N. Potter, 1963). See also Robert Theobald, *An Alternative Future for America II* (Chicago: The Swallow Press, 1970), pp. 116–17. Here he revises his 1963 guaranteed income plan. $1,400 would be guaranteed to every adult and $900 to every child. There would be no income tax exemptions, and most deductions would be eliminated. All income from any other source would be taxed. He retains his Committed Spending Plan, too.

10. Edward E. Schwartz, "A Way to End the Means Test," *Social Work*, IX, 3 (July, 1964). See also, Edward E. Schwartz, "An End to the Means Test," in Robert Theobald, ed., *The Guaranteed Income* (Garden City, N.Y.: Anchor Books, Doubleday and Co., 1967).

11. U.S., Office of Economic Opportunity, *Preliminary Results of the New Jersey Graduated Work Incentive Experiment*, February 18, 1970.

12. *Ibid.*, p. 3. The first two conclusions are quoted. The third is paraphrased and combines information on pp. 3 and 23. See also, *The Milwaukee Journal*, May 9, 1971, p. 3.

Chapter 11

1. This is an analysis of FAP II as it was presented to the U.S. House of Representatives in June, 1971. Quite helpful has been The Center on

Notes

Social Welfare Policy and Law, Columbia University, *H.R. 1: The Opportunities for Families Program and Family Assistance Plan,* "A Comment on Amendments to the Aid to Families with Dependent Children Program Approved by the Committee on Ways and Means, U.S. House of Representatives," May, 1971.

2. U.S. Department of Health, Education and Welfare, Social and Rehabilitation Service, Nation Center for Social Statistics, Program Statistics and Data Systems, NCSS Report F-2 (FY 70), *Source of Funds Expended for Public Assistance Payments and for the Cost of Administration, Services, and Training, fiscal year ended June 30, 1970,* table 2. See also, Mayor John V. Lindsay, quoted in *The New York Times,* May 14, 1971, p. 51.

3. Center on Social Welfare Policy and Law, Columbia University, *H.R. 1: The Opportunities for Families,* pp. 30–31.

4. *The New York Times,* July 16, 1971, p. 12.